BEFORE
THE WORLD
WAS LOST

A JOURNEY TO EDEN

Karisa DeLay

Vendera
Publishing

Vendera Publishing
www.venderapublishing.com

First published 2019

ISBN: 978-1-936307-49-4 (Ingram Paperback)
ISBN: 978-1-936307-46-3 (Amazon Paperback)
ISBN: 978-1-936307-47-0 (eBook)

2 4 6 8 10 9 7 5 3 1

Cover Art by Tim Kruskamp with Silent Shudder Photography

Typeset and Design by Scribe Freelance Book Design Co.
www.scribefreelance.com

To find out more about our authors and books visit
www.venderapublishing.com. Here you will find extracts, author interviews,
details of forthcoming events and the option to sign up for our newsletters.

Vendera Publishing books may be purchased for business or promotional use.
For information on bulk purchases send an email to:
admin@venderapublishing.com.

TABLE OF

Contents

A Thin Line Between Science and Religion

"Science without religion is lame, religion without science is blind."
—*Albert Einstein*

MANKIND, GALAXIES, THE universe—when did it all REALLY begin? Would it change the way we perceive science if we found evidence to support the existence of God(s)? Or would we question our faith if we realized that the God(s) we seek resides deep in the center of the universe instead of living in a golden city floating on clouds with choruses of angels?

We can't answer when it all began, and I'm not sure it would change the way we look at everything if we could show an alternate path of truth that brought religion and science together. We are an intelligent species that has come up with many ideas about how our world came to be, both religiously and scientifically. However, history tells us that as we uncover new things about the world we live in, we either rethink what we believe to be truth and start a new religion, or we ignore anything that makes us question our God and stay blind to the doors God is opening for us.

As a child, I grew up around a variety of God-fearing people who tried to instill a faith of fear. I witnessed how these people believed they had to fear God if they uttered anything that questioned the Bible or doubted anything that was shouted from the pulpit, which made it difficult for my vivid imagination to get real answers to my list of doctrinal questions. I felt that I was missing important details from the Bible, and I had no direction. That's why I often spent my time at church services with my scriptures open and a notepad in hand to jot down how to either contradict the sermon being preached or find answers to the questions in my head. If you try to find solid answers in the Bible without direction and without understanding history, science, archeology, and other facets of this world, you can get lost in translation.

One Sunday after church, when I was thirteen, I asked the preacher, "If there is no beginning and no end, then why does the Bible say, 'In the beginning' and 'in the end of days?' And why doesn't the Bible talk about God creating the dinosaurs?"

My mother was embarrassed that I had asked such a strange question. The preacher, who was way more educated than my elementary mind, searched his brain to give me some kind of answer. His response, along with that of every preacher I asked, was, "You're too young to worry about things we aren't meant to know right now."

That moment led me to always search for real answers, especially pertaining to God. I didn't question "if" God existed, because somehow I knew there was a higher intelligence than us. It was the "how" that triggered my journey of searching for answers and brought me to write this book.

My path has led me through the doors of many traditional Protestant worship services, along with long conversations with some nontraditional worshippers. Looking back, I know God allowed me to walk this path of uncertainty to open my eyes to the ways other people see—or don't see—God, in order to one day find answers to the questions I had been asking for so long. He even led some awesome non-Christians into my life to help me appreciate other points of view regarding how we came into existence.

Creation isn't an easy topic to discuss without someone getting offended. It's a complex topic, one that seems to have endless possibilities, even the possibility that a superior being existed in the beginning and designed all that we see and can't see. Regrettably, this is an untestable statement, and merely stating it doesn't bring us any closer to knowing how our species got its start on this rotating rock.

One position we can all agree on is that we do tangibly exist. The part that gets blurry for some is whether or not we were a spontaneous mishap or a flawless design by some unseen being. For the latter to be true, we must have a physical starting point here on Earth. Thus my question as a child about the first line of the Bible: "In the beginning …"

Whether we are talking about the first day man was placed on this planet or the first day of everything in this universe, we couldn't possibly consider any answers as fact. We just can't. It's like trying to finish a jigsaw puzzle with no edge pieces and no picture to reference.

My favorite book in the Bible is Genesis, especially the first chapter. Questions about how the world was shaped and how man spread across the world drove my inner Indiana Jones. The pages in the beginning of my Bible were worn the most, and I had most of Genesis nearly memorized.

My second-favorite books to read when I was younger, other than the Bible, were books on The Big Bang, aliens, and mysterious places on Earth. I needed to understand the world outside of the Bible.

What did I learn? Both sides need faith.

There are holes in both scientific theories of creation and the divine creation story; that's why both sides are still up for debate. For example, many ancient texts have been tainted by retranslation for personal or political reasons, casting doubt on the accuracy of real events and leaving faithful believers conflicted, which can lead them to seeking without direction.

Adding to the confusion, science has taken what we know about our planet and made some plausible guesses about how it might have all been formed. The problem with religion looking to science for wisdom concerning creation lies with the timeline. Science establishes existence at billions of years, while overly translated religious texts leave us with a guess of under ten thousand, making agreement difficult.

How can we come together with one truth proving either that there is a God or that we derived out of nothing?

I asked myself this for years, knowing that my faith had me on one side of the fence but with the grass looking just as green on the other side. Each argument had its valid points regarding how we all got here. To tear down the fence and see religion and science as the same, we would have to show how they both fit within the same parameters.

The Big Bang gets a bad rap because most think it's an explanation of the universe's origins. In reality, it's a theory that explains what happened when the universe was in a tiny dense state and how it began to rapidly expand. The Big Bang doesn't explain what took place before the expansion or what is outside our universe. Thus, the Big Bang theory doesn't deny the existence of God(s). It is man who adds that element.

With creation via a God, we rely on written histories from ancient cultures handed down to posterity in hopes of preserving the history throughout the ages. Of course, it would have been easier if the ancients had kept their stories straight over the years, used less symbology, or left us the key to read their cave drawings. Imagine the disagreements over religious capitalism that could've been avoided. Since they didn't, we must find our way back, semi-blinded, through the variant versions created by the imaginations of men.

This seemed like fantasy to me until spring of 2012. After starting my first novel, *The Crystal Gate*, I sought for new inspiration through prayer. Instantly, I felt a prompting to fill a blank map with the places of mysterious origin and purpose. The more factors I added, the more I began to see a pattern. This brought me to a unique place on Earth, the possible Cradle of Life: the Garden of Eden.

After writing my first two novels and incorporating what I had found into the storyline, I decided to blog about the information in hopes of completing a timeline of what I had uncovered.

After sharing this information with MUFON and other sources, I learned how unique this theory was and how significant it may become.

The problem is that conversations involving religious-based subjects are often considered taboo, and no one wants to hear another side that may challenge their own view. Intermingling the discussion with science could end friendships or lead to being fitted for a straitjacket.

Due to the stereotypes we've given to science and religion, we look upon them as oil and water. Yet, neither has a true sense of what really happened in the beginning, and neither has proven their own case well enough to stand as solid truth.

As I said, both sides need faith.

The sciences generally steer toward the agnostic perspective of, "I'll believe it when I see it," versus the religious stance of, "I'll take everything on faith, who needs to see it?" Scientific theories don't put God into their equations to solve problems, because it's a factor that cannot be tested. Religion usually doesn't include science, because science questions the validity of an all-powerful God.

However, a small but growing number of people are beginning to see that there is no conflict between the knowledge of God(s) and the applications of science. This idea can give us more answers to the question of how it's possible for all to be under one umbrella, to live in a world where it's not odd to believe in God and Ancient Aliens or to understand how God's creation in the Bible parallels the Big Bang.

The crazy timeline of Earth and humans is what screws with everyone's mind. Even the idea that we all descended from two people to become a gene pool of billions of people who vary in color, shape, intelligence, and blood type is proof there has been a significant change from the original version of the story.

However, this doesn't necessarily knot us into an evolutionary chain that binds us to lesser species. It means that whoever created us used the same set of ingredients to create multiple recipes for life; it doesn't mean we descended from chimpanzees. Besides, if evolutionary theory is based on how much DNA different species have in common, then we might as well have our family reunions with cats or even fruit flies, with whom we share 60% DNA. The point is that this planet is connected, but we are way too complex to not have a superior intelligence beyond our imaginations.

History seems to repeat itself, and notions about our origins resulted from continuously allowing our brains to be reprogrammed by the words of men, who believed the words of men passed along to them by other men as the truth, and so on down through the generations until symbolic stories became the "facts" on which our beliefs are based. We get no closer to finding the answers by guessing. Each time the scriptures were translated or simplified, to help bring more people to an understanding, it diluted the line of organized truth.

I'm not discrediting the power of the stories told in the scriptures. Those stories can still give mankind hope of joy, strength, purpose, and life after death. But the exact meanings of where we came from, where God resides, and where we will go beyond the grave have missing pieces that separate our world into different belief systems.

We have lost the connection between the "where" and the "why" of who we are, because we refuse to accept truths from more than one side. This universe is larger than we can comprehend in this lifetime, but the clues to piecing together how we fit within the unseeable walls are right here on Earth. We need to open our eyes to let our hearts and minds work together to trust that God, the original scientist, who knows the desires of our wondering, would not leave us empty-handed or without a path to find answers. We need to uncover the world as it was before it was lost by man.

This book is not an argument to disprove science or a claim that there is no need for science with a God. We cannot prove that God exists any more than we can prove scientific theories about how we came into existence. You can hold to one and stay blinded, because all Creation stories have room for discrediting. For example, the Big Bang theory is left with many holes that theorists have yet to explain, and yet people take the gaps of understanding on faith. The more that science and religion collaborate, the closer we are to filling in those spaces and seeing the God who has been looking at us through the ultimate telescope.

Faith is what it is, a belief in things unseen or unproven, and it doesn't discriminate between science or religion. Beyond finding a simple pattern on a map, my mind was opened to piece together the information I had been gathering since I was very young. Therefore, we will take this journey through the scriptural stories, historical texts, archeological landmarks, and other scientific theories that have guided me to evidence that reveals some of our missing treasures in the world. Things that at one point seemed random will now begin to link the pieces of a bigger picture. The next chapters require an open mind and a willingness to relearn what we thought we knew in hopes of finding history before it was written.

CHAPTER I

The Line from the Paranormal to God

"We dismiss the possibility of what may be,
because we fear what we might learn."
—Anonymous

OUR WORLD HAS become saturated with swaying evidence of the paranormal, the extraterrestrial, and the unexplained, including evidence of a higher power. It would be nearly impossible to sort through all the personal witnessing, determine the validity of all the disembodied voices caught electronically, authenticate the photos of ghost-like beings walking through the shadows, debunk the questionable UFOs filmed over rooftops, weigh the countless sightings of Bigfoot, and try to verify all the claims of the presence of angels, especially with advanced technology that can make things appear real.

Regardless, many of us, myself included, have had some sort of paranormal experience in our lifetime, one that we felt was 100 percent real and unexplainable.

My first experience came at a slumber party when I was eight years old. It was so vivid and real, I remember it like it was yesterday. Seven girls headed into the living room to get ready to fall asleep. I was the last one into the room, thus I was responsible for turning out the kitchen lights. As I did, I turned to my right to see a small black child no taller than three feet, dressed in a simple blue dress with a white apron. I instantly ran to the couch and turned back to see if someone else was coming down the hall, but the hallway was empty. No one else was there, and no one else in the house was awake aside from us seven girls. My imagination wasn't overreacting, I know what I saw, just like so many others who've had similar experiences.

It's hard to deny that we are surrounded by mysteries that seem to be unconnected. Yet, when you throw the existence of a superior being into the universal mix, shouldn't it lead one to believe that all the strange occurrences would fit within the parameters of a divine design? If one can believe in a divine power that knows all and created all, then why are stories of the paranormal farfetched?

Let us begin with our friendly ghosts.

Who or what are they?

The presence of spirits in the afterlife is not a modern phenomenon. Ghosts are the most widely believed phenomena of the paranormal world, without regard to faith or nationality. Much of the recent popularity of the spirit world comes from the pseudoscience of ghost hunting. If you've missed this trend, it's easily found all over the internet, with vlogs and television investigation shows, which proves you don't need a real science education to study or hunt ghosts.

Equipped with just a few high-tech gadgets and a hand-held voice recorder, anyone can become a ghost hunter. However, all this hype creates a glut of evidence. Now every speck of dust is believed at first to be a ghost.

I am not trying to discredit all witnesses, since I have experienced a ghostly encounter of my own. We just need to separate the Hollywood versions from what's really happening.

Typically, most styles of paranormal study have standards that investigators follow to find proof of ghosts. Techniques include using EVP recorders to detect and record electronic voice phenomena, EMF recorders to sense fluctuations in electromagnetic fields, thermal imaging for detecting unique temperature signatures, and 3D imaging software to map the outlines of anomalies.

What makes these tools great is that the information is received without much human error. The hypothesis that most investigators stand on is that ghosts feed off of some form of energy (heat, electromagnetic, human emotion, etc.). With this underpinning, they try to prove that there is more than what our eyes allow us to see.

It is thought that there are different types of haunting categories and that each is based on the intelligence of the spirit (residual, interactive, poltergeist, demonic, shadows, and the double walkers). Since no one has produced any irrefutable evidence, this is purely a model of a science that has yet to be authenticated.

Before technology, there were people who supported belief in the existence of spirits (or ghosts) living on after death. Some even propose that it can be explained by physics. Albert Einstein, theoretical physicist, is believed to have suggested a scientific basis for ghosts. He stated that energy cannot be created or destroyed, but only change form. This is the law of conservation of energy, also known as thermodynamics. This law would only make sense if one believes that a human has both a physical and spiritual energy to make up their total energy, and when the physical part dies the other remains after death.

Could this explain what happens to our energy when we die? That our spiritual energy, or life force, is what makes up the ghost realm? A typical scientist would probably say no and tell you that basic physics says your energy goes back into the environment and that no viable intelligent energy is left behind to be detected by paranormal hunting parties—but I'm no scientist. I can see past the brick walls that stop the thinking process of some. If men had kept thinking of absolute impossibilities we wouldn't have discovered DNA, antibiotics, or much of anything in the 1900s.

I don't fault brilliant scientists; they are trained to only accept hypotheses based on testing in controlled environments. Therefore, they state that ghosts are not real because they can't reproduce the evidence. Also, since we haven't caught an authentic spiritual being and sat it down for an interview as an authority on the subject, how do we know if ghosts are real? The answer is simple: history. By searching ancient texts as well as the pre-technology era for witness accounts, we can find the answers we seek.

Intriguingly, the folklore of spirits, or the ghostly dead, harks back to some of the oldest writings found. Specific beliefs about the afterlife vary within cultures, but there are constants that agree that the dead live past their physical end. For example, most believed that a realm (or place) exists for the spirits to reside and that this spiritual realm is governed by immutable laws that assured that the dead remained there unless the God(s) allowed them to return.

Most did not welcome a spirit's return. A ghostly presence in the land of the living meant the spirit had unfinished business, such as last funeral rites, improper burial, a missing body, or a traumatic death such as murder or suicide, prompting the dead to seek revenge. If true, this could further validate the claims of ghost hunters that they feel emotions during their investigations.

Such hauntings can occur after all manner of death—other than dying in your sleep at an old age—which may explain how it's possible for these spirits to choose to return. This continued opposition between life and what happens after death is an ambivalence resulting from where we as humans stand in faith. Our faiths can leave us afraid to believe in ghosts yet too scared not to have hope in an afterlife.

Many turn to religious teachings in books such as the Bible to understand what happens to one's spirit after death. And what does the Bible tell us about a realm of spirits in the world after death? *(All biblical references will come from the KJV)*

LUKE 16:19-31

19 There was a certain rich man, which was clothed in purple and fine linen, and fared sumptuously every day:

20 And there was a certain beggar named Lazarus, which was laid at his gate, full of sores, 21 And desiring to be fed with the crumbs which fell from the rich man's table: moreover the dogs came and licked his sores.

22 And it came to pass, that the beggar died, and was carried by the angels into Abraham's bosom: the rich man also died, and was buried; 23 And in hell he lift up his eyes, being in torments, and seeth Abraham afar off, and Lazarus in his bosom.

24 And he cried and said, Father Abraham, have mercy on me, and send Lazarus, that he may dip the tip of his finger in water, and cool my tongue; for I am tormented in this flame.

25 But Abraham said, Son, remember that thou in thy

lifetime receivedst thy good things, and likewise Lazarus evil things: but now he is comforted, and thou art tormented.

[26] And beside all this, between us and you there is a great gulf fixed: so that they which would pass from hence to you cannot; neither can they pass to us, that would come from thence.

[27] Then he said, I pray thee therefore, father, that thou wouldest send him to my father's house: [28] For I have five brethren; that he may testify unto them, lest they also come into this place of torment.

[29] Abraham saith unto him, They have Moses and the prophets; let them hear them.

[30] And he said, Nay, father Abraham: but if one went unto them from the dead, they will repent. [31] And he said unto him, If they hear not Moses and the prophets, neither will they be persuaded, though one rose from the dead.

Here, Christ is teaching about two men's deaths, speaking about how each man was separated by a great gulf. One was in the torment of hell asking for the other to help him. These verses not only suggest that there is life after death but also show that the dead are aware and intelligent enough to seek help from those not in the torments of hell, implying that one could escape the wrath of such hell even after death. So maybe "death" is only the beginning.

FURTHER IN LUKE 23:42 – 43:

[42] And he said unto Jesus, Lord, remember me when thou comest into thy kingdom.

[43] And Jesus said unto him, Verily I say unto thee, Today shalt thou be with me in paradise.

As Christ neared the sixth hour on the cross, one of the criminals that was nailed alongside him asked to be remembered by Jesus in Heaven after death. Christ says, "Verily I say unto thee, today shalt thou be with me in paradise." This is my favorite reference to what happens after we pass through the veil of death. Anyone who knows the story of Christ's journey after he dies on the cross knows he did not immediately go to Heaven where his Father resides. Thus, the celebration of Easter three days later. In fact, he must have visited another realm of paradise where he had promised the man he would be. This is evident in 1 Peter 3:18-19, when the scriptures compare Christ's death in the flesh before being quickened by the Spirit so he could preach to the spirits in prison.

Once again, this paradise place goes back to the first scriptural reference about the two men separated by a great gulf and the level of existence needed after death to allow coherent learning.

The Bible continues to add clues about a spiritual world by telling us that three days later, after the proclaimed resurrection, Christ told Mary in the garden (John 20:17) not to touch him for he had not ascended unto his Father. Later, Jesus walked through closed doors (John 20:26). Aside from the religious aspect of this miraculous resurrection, the amazing thing about these verses is clear language suggesting that we don't leave our bodies and go directly to Heaven to be cut off from the Earth. Instead, we go to a place where Christ had gone to preach to the dead, a place where a paradise and a land of torment can exist, a place here on Earth.

Not everyone seeks answers from the leftover remnants of the Bible, but that doesn't mean there is no common ground on the issue of life after death within the Christian tradition. For the most part, the Jewish and Islamic faiths concur; they are in agreement that the souls of the righteous go to a place like the Bible's version of paradise, where the dead will be waiting to be resurrected after the coming of their God.

Moreover, both Judaism and Islam agree on the tormenting nature of some type of hell, according to one's actions in the flesh. These and other faiths' reasons for disagreements derive from the identity of who their God truly is or isn't and whether he has already been here or not. (Good thing this book isn't touching that subject.)

The point, however, is that as different as religions appear to be, there is sometimes common ground to work from to help explain concrete topics like our creation, our physical death, and what happens to our essence when we pass, as well as whether our actions decide which side of the river we end up on. If we agree there is life beyond the grave, then we can almost agree there is a God, a source of positive energy. That means we also have to face the existence of an opposite side of that energy.

Which brings us to the darker side of spirits and ghosts. Most eyewitness accounts of hauntings, or spiritual activity, do not report a good source. If you believe there is a God(s) who is of pure light, you would agree that there is a power source for the darkness, making the

Devil also real. If he was cast from Heaven, as said in Revelation 12, then so were the angels that came with him.

The Bible teaches us that one-third of the host of Heaven fell with the devil to Earth (Rev. 12:4). We don't need a lot examples of scriptures stating that demons roam freely on this planet causing havoc, but Matthew 8:28-32 shows that it is possible for demons to possess humans to confuse and interfere with us:

MATTHEW 8:28 – 32

28 And when he was come to the other side into the country of the Gergesenes, there met him two possessed with devils, coming out of the tombs, exceeding fierce, so that no man might pass by that way.

29 And, behold, they cried out, saying, What have we to do with thee, Jesus, thou Son of God? Art thou come hither to torment us before the time?

30 And there was a good way off from them an herd of many swine feeding.

31 So the devils besought him, saying, If thou cast us out, suffer us to go away into the herd of swine.

32 And he said unto them, Go. And when they were come out, they went into the herd of swine: and, behold, the whole herd of swine ran violently down a steep place into the sea, and perished in the waters.

This makes sense when the bottom line for most wars and culture differences is what each of us believes, especially about our morality, through which we get to the paradise of the afterlife.

In the modern West, near the rainforests of the Amazon, we can find the Yanomami people, or Sanema, and we will learn of their deep-rooted beliefs in how nature and the spirit are working as one. Of course, each tribal group has its own creation myth and beliefs that were passed down orally from generation to generation, causing variances. However, the basic belief of the people, known as shamanism, is that all things are unified by spiritual workings. Nature and spirit are not only one in the workings around them, but the fate of humanity and the fate of the earth are linked as one—if you destroy the environment, then you destroy life.

Their leaders, or shamans, speak of the universe containing four layers: a top layer, where the ancients once resided before they dropped down; a sky layer where dead spirits reside; the earthly layer for humans; and an underworld where ancient spirits bring misfortune to the people of earth. The Yanomami tribes perform hallucination rituals in order to enter the layers that hold both good and bad spirits.

Here are the parts I find intriguing: We have a culture of people located deep in the Amazon forest that experienced very little outside influence until the 1970s. Yet they claim to have a great understanding of how interdimensional spirits can interact with the living. Much can be said about the simplicity of their practices, but their advanced thought about communication with the dead is easily paired with our modern pseudoscience of ghost hunting. They don't have Photoshop to enhance an image to make it look like ghosts are present; they believe they can literally intermingle with them.

The other intriguing part is how their notion of layers in the universe is much like what Paul taught to the Corinthians when he mentioned the different times of bodies. Paul is very descriptive about how everything has its own flesh, or its own glory from God. This reference displays how this vast universe was understood by the followers of Christ, even the separation of earth from the terrestrial space and the celestial heavens. He further separates the natural body from the spiritual one.

1 CORINTHIANS 15:39 – 44

[39] *All flesh is not the same flesh: but there is one kind of flesh of men, another flesh of beasts, another of fishes, and another of birds.*

[40] *There are also celestial bodies, and bodies terrestrial: but the glory of the celestial is one, and the glory of the terrestrial is another.*

[41] *There is one glory of the sun, and another glory of the moon, and another glory of the stars: for one star differeth from another star in glory.*

[42] *So also is the resurrection of the dead. It is sown in corruption; it is raised in incorruption:*

[43] *It is sown in dishonour; it is raised in glory: it is sown in weakness; it is raised in power:* [44] *It is sown a natural body; it is raised a spiritual body. There is a natural body, and there is a spiritual body.*

Though people disagree on where we came from and where we

are going, it doesn't change the fact that something happens after we die. Once our physical body is done and the energy within us goes on, that energy is believed by the pseudoscience of ghost hunting to be detectable.

With the rise of the internet and increased interest in ghost hunting, people are documenting more and more cases of repeated hauntings all over the world. Taking into account that a lot of the claims can be false, there is something to be said about worldwide witnessing of similar occurrences that have been around since before technology.

The following map is a representation of some of the most reported areas for spiritual activity, or ghostly activity, around the world. This doesn't represent all of the areas of claimed hauntings, only areas considered hotspots for such repeated presences. Keep in mind the small pattern in which these hotspots are located as we move on.

Areas with the most repeated reports of haunted activity

This map may appear to be a bunch of random dots, but this was compiled from multiple sources reporting repeated ghost sightings. These dots represent a central point for more than one location in that area. Many of the places denoted on this map are known for their high amounts of testable electromagnetic energy and sheer creepy feelings. Why is that important? Maybe these spots have a force pulling ghostly spirits or dark entities to them, or maybe the energy is drawing them. Either way, these areas are also known for other unexplained phenomena, and as we move to the next chapter, the significance of these places to our uncertain history will begin to make sense.

DEUTERONOMY 29:29

[29] The secret things belong unto the LORD our God: but those things which are revealed belong unto us and to our children for ever, that we may do all the words of this law.

The scriptures of God(s) have given us a foundation, and the technology of man has brought us closer to seeing what Creation truly looks like. Our arguments pit the pages of Adam against the theory of atoms, but as we look through telescopes we realize we are all here together and there is much we don't know.

CHAPTER II

The Line from Science Fiction to Reality

"Fiction reveals truth that reality obscures."
—Ralph Waldo Emerson

SINCE THE FIRST foot touched the dust of the moon's surface, we have become more fascinated with traveling among the stars and exploring other planets for possible life. We have telescopes that can see galaxies light years away and probes that can travel to nearby planets to test their atmospheres for potential habitation.

We have developed sciences within sciences as our understanding becomes more complicated. We can see—and even travel—greater distances through the universe than we had dreamed of a century ago.

Which raises a question: If you were on the other side of the telescope standing with God(s), and you could see past the heavenly clouds and all the planets, would you not think there is another race of beings living in one of the multitude of galaxies out in the universe your God(s) created? Or do you think these galaxies were created merely to take up space? It's doubtful an immortal God(s) would waste their time. They have a purpose, and more than likely put life on one of their other beautiful creations.

Believing that intelligent life exists only on Earth is no different from thinking that we are a product of evolution and everything happened by chance. If there is "alien" life past our atmosphere, then it gives less validation to evolution and more evidence that a superior creator is out there creating beings like humans. Before we decide to shut people down for looking toward the skies for aliens, let's see what the Christian Bible tells us. Genesis 1:26-27 tells us that the God(s) in charge wanted man to look like them, which leaves room to think that beings on other planets may not look like us.

GENESIS 1:26 – 27

26 And God said, Let us make man in our image, after our likeness: and let them have dominion over the fish of the sea, and over the fowl of the air, and over the cattle, and over all the earth, and over every creeping thing that creepeth upon the earth.

27 So God created man in his own image, in the image of God created he him; male and female created he them.

Plus, we are given clues about other worlds:

HEBREWS 1:2,

2 Hath in these last days spoken unto us by his Son, whom he hath appointed heir of all things, by whom also he made the worlds;

The Apostle Paul understood creation, especially since he learned from the Son of God who was given reign over all things, including the "worlds" he created by this power. Most of the Bible speaks with poetry and symbolism to leave the reader to ponder and seek meaning through prayer. It's understandable that one cannot simply search the words "alien" or "extraterrestrial" and expect to find answers to whether they exist.

However, there are plenty of clues that indicate cosmic travel and suggest that other beings have visited Earth throughout our history to help humans. Not everyone will experience an alien, angelic, or ghostly encounter or any that doesn't appear natural. It's not necessary to witness beings from out of this world to comprehend the feeling of not being alone. We can look at the vastness of just our massive galaxy to see the potential for endless life.

At the age of thirteen, my eyes were opened to the fact that we are not alone. One night, I was staying at my grandparents' home in the countryside of southern Ohio. After lying in bed unable to sleep, I went to the living room to watch a show until I fell asleep. Before I could turn the television on, I saw through the window a large green ball of light slowly brushing over the treetops. There was no sound and no extra wind to move the branches. My family didn't believe me until two days later, when the local paper mentioned others who had witnessed the same phenomenon that night. Since then, I have seen strange lights in the sky a couple of times on the way to my grandparents' house.

Over the years, both experts and amateurs in the field of ufology have wondered why UFO sightings, for the most part, seem random. Most of these encounters are seen over unique places of interest, such as Stonehenge, the Nazca Lines, military bases, and several bodies of water. These reported sightings are investigated by ufologists and groups like MUFON (Mutual UFO Network), which keep data from these strange events.

Luckily for us, these groups keep excellent records of where most of these sightings appear. The following is a map of UFO hotspots reported from 1947-2007. It shows data from more than 114,000 UFO sightings, including precise geographic location information available from over 90,000 cases. The lighter grey areas are uninhabited; dark grey areas are inhabited. This shows the population differences among places where sightings have been reported, which are represented by black dots.

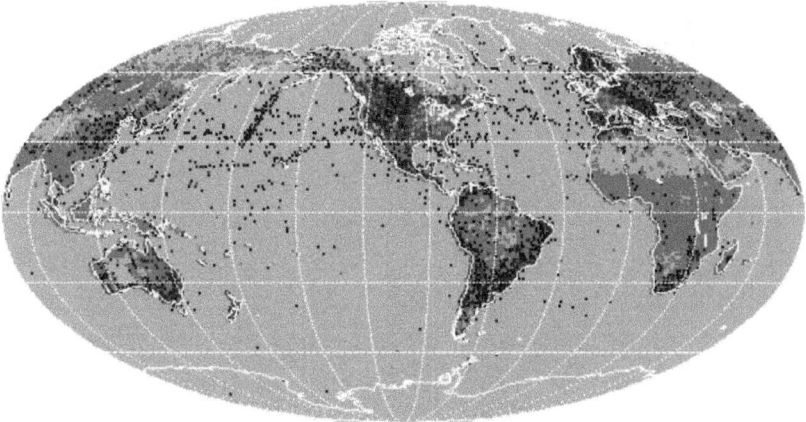

Reported UFO sightings, 1947-2007

This first map illustrates multiple sightings but doesn't isolate areas where repeated sightings happened throughout those years. Neither does it show where these UFOs were headed after the original sightings. Many of the reported sightings could be spots where UFOs entered the atmosphere, indicating flight paths rather than destinations.

The next map displays areas that have been recorded as hotspots for UFO or alien sightings. Sightings of UFOs are described typically as having super speed and round or saucer-like shapes; however, they're also known for their ability to hover in midair with little to no sound. These dots are more likely the destinations of these unidentified objects, since the areas noted had multiple sightings reported over the years.

Areas with repeated UFO sightings

Notice the pattern on this map. The concentrations are similar to those of the ghost hot spots map. The next map shows them overlapping. Black denotes the UFO hotspots and grey denotes the reported haunted hotspots. The overlap is not a coincidence; there is something unique about these areas.

Overlap of UFOs and haunted areas

How do we fit aliens into our belief system? Why are they coming to Earth? Are they friendly? Do they have the same free will as we do? Are their God(s) the same as ours? I can't show proof to answer these questions, but I believe they have the same God we do, and that they are here because of what sets Earth apart from the other planets. In the next chapter I will show you what they could be looking for when they visit and how it ties into finding the Garden of Eden. There are plenty of strange sightings of ghosts and aliens, but not all mysterious things are beings we can't tangibly catch.

There are plenty of places around the world that leave us scratching our heads—Stonehenge, Easter Island (site of the famous stone statues called *moai*), and the Nazca Desert in southern Peru (site of the Nazca Lines) top most lists. Stonehenge is familiar because of its recognizable circular formation of megalithic stones, but it is not alone. Over a thousand surviving examples of stone structures are scattered across the UK and around the globe. The next map shows the countries in which these stone circle formations and large stones, known also as menhirs, are located.

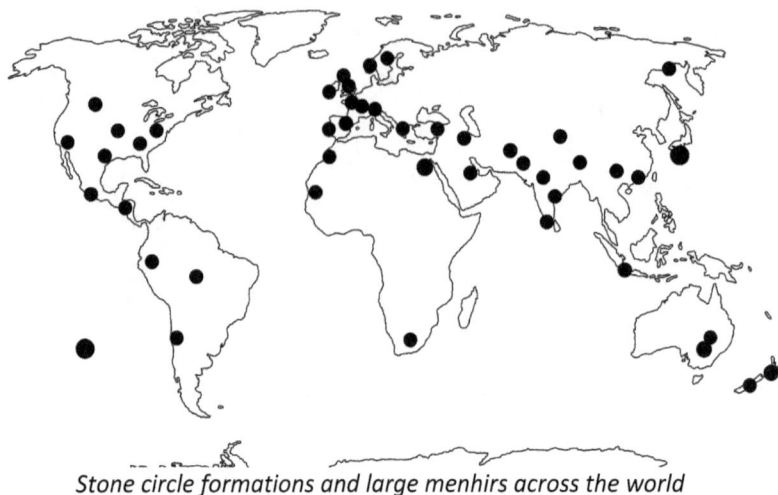

Stone circle formations and large menhirs across the world

This map does not detail the exact locations of every stone structure but rather the central point of where they are referenced. For example, more than a thousand stone circles that survive across the British Isles couldn't individually fit on this map. The key here is not the amount but the location.

The captivating part of these structures is not just their large mass, which would require a multitude of men to lift and shape them, or the fact that most of the stones came from miles away. What's fascinating is the arrangement of these stones and how they seem to align with something more cosmic, or even spiritual.

Stonehenge, Wiltshire, England

Göbekli Tepe, Turkey

Drombeg stones, Ireland

Taulas of Menorca, Spain

Notions about their placement range from sacred burial grounds and healing sites to celestial observatories and sound stages. There is no testable way to know why the ancient people erected these structures; we can only guess.

Aside from their placement coinciding with the pathway of haunting hot spots and UFO sightings, this abundance of similar building shows a global connection. Australia has even been working on uncovering an ancient stone formation of its own.

Digital rendering of stone formation near Mullumbimby, Australia
(image credit Richard Andrew Patterson)

The world is filled with strange, unexplainable mysteries. Places in South America like the gigantic outline drawings of the Nazca Lines in Peru or the *moai* monolith statues on a tiny speck of an island west of Peru called Rapa Nui (also known as Easter Island) keep us wondering about their creators. Additional sites include the mega city of Teotihuacan, the other deserted civilizations of Central America, the Egyptian pyramids, and all the other unexplained mounds built across the world. These raise many questions about their purpose. Even the site of Göbekli Tepe in Turkey, which predates the Great Pyramids by thousands of years, gives us pause in understanding the ancient people of our Earth. These and many other places leave us stranded without many clues, only guesses. The following images show some less popular sites of prehistoric mound building that are similar to other pyramid bases.

Monks Mound in Illinois (base size similar to the Great Pyramid of Giza)

Monks Mound, which is east of St. Louis, Missouri, in the United States, is one of the largest pre-Columbian earthworks in the Americas. It looks like the base of a pyramid. It is not only located in North America, a mile from the Mississippi River, but also was built with nonlocal materials almost 5,000 years ago. In addition, this 14.4-acre space (92Hx951Dx836W) consists of more than an estimated

2.16 billion pounds of nonlocal soil types. Along with cypress and red cedar posts and limestone slabs, Monks Mound used soil not found in the surrounding floodplain.

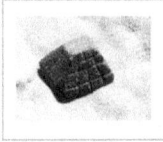

A pyramid stone found in the Greenville-Sorento, Illinois, area. It was described as a flat-topped mound, it is smooth on two of the sloping sides, and the other two have cross-hatching and some unknown symbol.

It not only would take a lot of time but also would require a lot of people to build a structure of this size. To accomplish it in under two years would require about 20,000 people unloading 50 pounds every second nonstop. And they had to travel great distances to get the soil. The original locations of the multiple soils found on this site are still being researched, but it's interesting that soil from an outside source was needed. It's as if the builders knew the waters were going to rise and were preparing for a flood.

The Gympie site has sparked interest. It predates colonial history and could be Egyptian, South American, or Chinese, but no one can say for sure. Some believe it was built for alien spacecraft, while others think it was made by early European immigrants for agriculture.

*Gympie Pyramid
in Australia*

Pyramid made of shells in Brazil

Most people associate pyramids with the Egyptian ones, built with stone blocks and no steps. But the once overlooked pyramids in Brazil were created from seashells and are older than the pyramids in Egypt. Though an ocean apart, the knowledge more than likely came from the same source. The next map shows where pyramids and pyramid-like structures exist around the world.

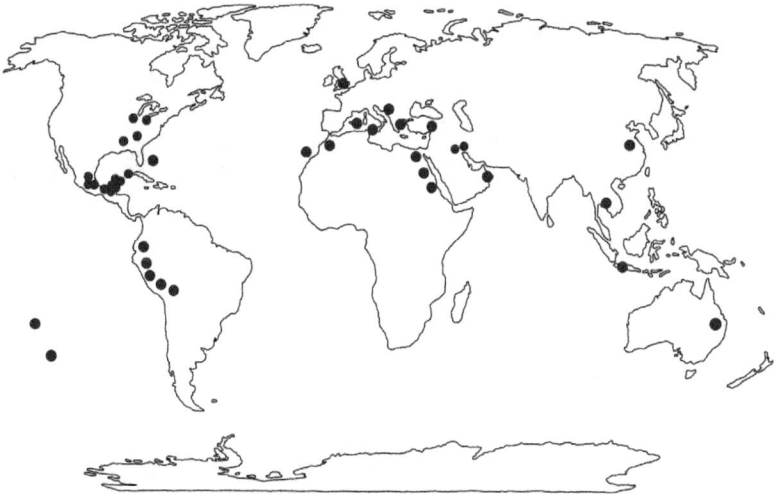

How various civilizations were able to create advanced architectural wonders like pyramids, step-pyramids, mound-like pyramids, and mounds remains an unanswered question. Intricate stones left behind by ancient cultures provide evidence that the world started with more knowledge than we once thought. Take the following places for example:

Ggantija on the Maltese island of Gozo

In Malta lies the second-oldest manmade structure, Ggantija. Roughly 5,500 years old, these encased oval ruins remain in fairly decent shape since their excavation in 1827. This location is about a two-day journey from the oldest known archaeological site, Göbekli Tepe, in Turkey.

The zig-zag base of Sacsayhuaman in Cusco, Peru

Aerial view of Sacsayhuaman

Located 12,000 feet above sea level, Sacsayhuaman has overlooked the city of Cusco for more than 1,100 years. Once again, there is much guessing about this structure's purpose. In the image above, Sacsayhuaman appears to be the remains of a very detailed building, possibly a temple, with a circle chamber placed in the center.

Different sets of steps located in Tiwanaku in Bolivia

Tiwanaku is a large area with several structures that have been uncovered by researchers over the years. Some think the area started as an agricultural settlement that grew to great numbers from around 300 B.C. to 300 A.D. One of the areas uncovered is Puma Punku.

Stonework from Puma Punku in Tiahuanaco, Bolivia.

Puma Punku, located in Tiahuanaco, Bolivia, is one of the more intriguing ancient building sites on the planet. At first glance these stones are not so different from other large ruins covering the planet during this time period. A closer look reveals stonework so precise that it shows no evidence of tool markings. With right angles that are smooth like marble and interlock perfectly, it's as though these stones were machined or created with a laser.

How were these advanced techniques accomplished without outside knowledge? The jury is still out, but theories about aliens seem more plausible.

Another out of place find is at Tiahuanaco, where T-shaped clamps were used to possibly interlock stones. It's unclear if these clamps were ceremonial pieces or were made to join together megaliths, but the ability of ancient cultures to create temperatures hot enough to melt such alloys again confounds our understanding of these people. The following image shows an iron clamp on the Tomb of King Remhai.

Tomb of King Remhai in Ethiopia

One thing is for certain, this knowledge was known across the globe. The next image shows how the knowledge of ancient clamps was used across the globe during the same timeline, just like the knowledge of pyramids.

When I first began researching archeological sites, they seemed to appear where a lot of the high concentrations of the unknown kept showing up. One might assume these places correspond with population, but that's not the case. The places where people take up residence are hit or miss with the previous maps.

The world's population density in 1994
(map source, United States Department of Agriculture)

The world's population density in 2015

Taking into consideration the areas of population density in North America, the western areas of South America, Europe into South Asia (India and China), and the edges of southeastern Australia up into Japan, it would make sense that the large number of people would result in a high number of witnesses of UFOs and ghost sightings. However, this doesn't explain why the other areas of dense population, such as the eastern coast of South America, the middle to southern areas of Africa, and northeast Europe and Russia have fewer reports and no remnants of ancient advanced cultures.

Easter Island, off the west coast of Chile, lies in the middle of the ocean and is barely inhabited. Why does it have high volumes of the paranormal, and why is it home to some very large and mysterious megalithic sculptures?

Statues of Easter Island (Rapa Nui)

Named by a Dutch explorer who arrived there on Easter Sunday of 1722, Easter Island has been visited by curious citizens of many countries but has been an annex of Chile, 2,300 miles away, since the late 19th century. The mystery of the statues, called *moai*, baffles us to this day. The island emerged from the ocean through multiple volcanic eruptions, a common phenomenon. Besides its gigantic statures, Easter Island is home to continuous alien sightings, ghost stories, and other legends that keep its economy booming with tourism.

Intriguing places like Easter Island, Puma Punku, Göbekli Tepe and other amazing landmarks with ancient puzzling architecture once had a purpose that their ancient inhabitants believed could be magnified with carefully laid-out architecture. We assume each place had a different culture, but what if their purpose was the same and only their forms of expression were different? The points on the previous maps about ghosts and aliens line up with the sites of these ancient structures, so what are they telling us? Based on their current positions, it doesn't seem like much, especially since they don't connect at any real point but are separated by oceans and mountain ranges. These places are real and important to whoever is visiting them—even if they're not from this world. These places have a kind of energy, a special kind of significance, that produces these unexplained sightings and continuously draws visitors.

An abundance of disparate beliefs separates the world and keeps us from knowing how everything is connected. Humans are stubborn when it comes to looking past their own piece of the puzzle, and therefore we remain separated from reality. Thinking we know everything is where we are wrong, and if together we can look at the world as a whole, we can journey back to where it all started and find the real Eden.

CHAPTER III

Putting the Pieces Together

"The pieces of the puzzle have a tendency to
come together when you least expect it."
—*Jane Green*

IF YOU BELIEVE humans started somewhere on Earth, you also believe
we migrated from our original location to spread across the world. The
challenge lies in deciding where we place the pin dot of our origin.
There is evidence that human life began in South Africa, Mesopotamia,
or even Australia. Whether we were placed there by the God(s) we
worship or by an ancient alien culture, or we spontaneously decided to
walk upright, life began somewhere.

With humans spread across a world separated by oceans, it is
difficult to see how we made it this far, but Earth didn't always look
like it does today. It was once a lot easier to trek from North America
to Indonesia. In school, most of us were asked to cut out the seven
continents and rearrange the pieces like a puzzle to form one landmass,
also known as Pangea. Looking at how the continents fit perfectly
together tells us that where our continents are now is not where they
started, and science tells us that the migration happened over a great
duration of time, before humans were on the planet. The evidence,
though, tells us something different.

For a long time it has been understood that the Earth didn't originally have seven continents, but instead one large mass of land and one great big ocean. The theory is that Earth is broken into "tectonic plates," which slid around over millions of years and placed the continents where they are today. Over a century ago, a scientist named Alfred Wegener proposed the theory of Pangea. Geologic records showed similar timeline compositions in coal deposits in Pennsylvania and Europe, meaning at one point they were close to each other. Mountain chains seem to connect to their counterparts across the ocean, more evidence of Pangea.

It was once believed that the center of Pangea would have been terribly dry, like a desert, but coal deposits form when plants and animals decay in swampy water. Thus, the theory changed. In 2016, researchers used data from fossil soils to reconstruct the ecosystem and climate during the time of Pangea. Researchers agreed that the land flourished with vegetation and possibly with living creatures.

The creation story doesn't spell out Pangea, but hints suggest there was one land mass, later separated into nations. Genesis 1:9 states the waters were gathered unto one place, which would leave the land equally gathered in one spot. Genesis 10:25 gives the generations of the sons and adds that the Earth was divided in Peleg's day. This could be a dividing of cultures, but that isn't likely since Genesis 10:5 told us of the nations' dividing.

GENESIS 1:9

⁹ And God said, Let the waters under the heaven be gathered together unto one place, and let the dry land appear: and it was so

GENESIS 10:25,

²⁵ And unto Eber were born two sons: the name of one was Peleg; for in his days was the earth divided; and his brother's name was Joktan.

GENESIS 10:5,

⁵ By these were the isles of the Gentiles divided in their lands; every one after his tongue, after their families, in their nations.

The next images show two different renderings of Pangea, illustrating where the continents might have been connected. Since we

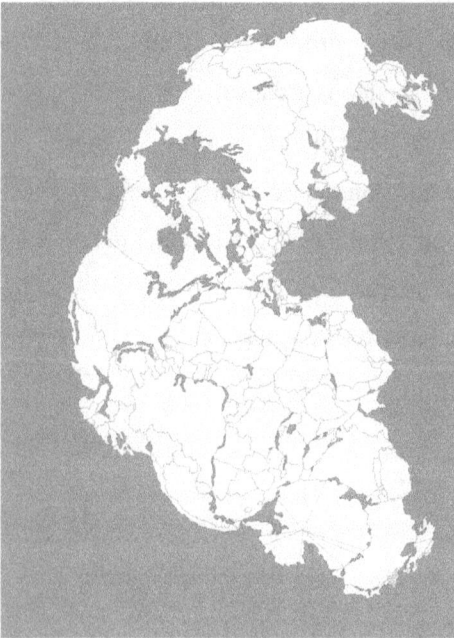

are still learning what the ocean floor looks like, these are all guesses and purely from the artist's viewpoint, not an exact scale. This provides a visual reference to where the pieces of the continents interlock. Some countries, like India, might have originally been divided and in separate places on Pangea.

Pangea with outlines of countries and a few capital cities

On the next image, the larger dots on the map of Pangea denote multiple site overlaps, or higher concentrations, given from the hotspots for UFOs, ghosts, circle formations, pyramids, and iron technology.

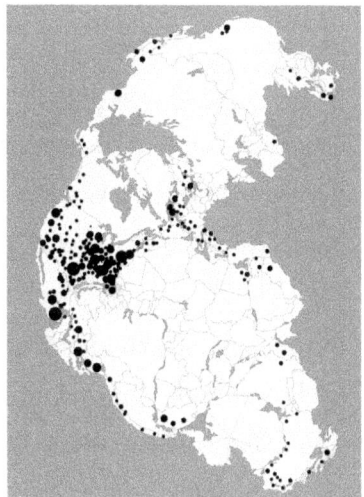

Pangea plotted location areas from the maps in Chapter 1 & 2

When the information from the previous chapters is added to Pangea, lines that seemed random now seem to have a connection. It appears that all the dotted lines touch together, with a common source in North America.

Any number of theories might explain this, but it might indicate a pathway of migration that prehistoric humans took after their start on Earth, contrary to popular belief.

These areas may still seem insignificant to our origins, but when you consider how everything branches out from North America and leads out across the globe, it starts to open the platform to new theories. Think about it. What do we know about ancient North America? Nothing, because no one thinks life started here. We still believe that the Indians were the first civilizations to relocate to this part of the world.

Theories can change or grow with additional understanding, just as the belief that Pangea was once covered mostly by deserts changed. What's accepted as fact today can change with additional data tomorrow.

These areas are frequently visited by otherworldly beings, haunted by spirits of the past, and left with remnants of former cultures. As soon as I put Pangea together with all the plotted points, my eyes were opened to the four distinct pathways, or the four rivers mentioned in the old Jewish texts. Could this be Eden? Could Eden have existed in North America? It started to come full circle. America is known as the New World, not the ancient world, but in reality it's all been here since the beginning. Who knows what truths lie beneath the surface of a land overlooked by archeology because of what little time man would've spent here before the flood?

I believe in a place called Eden, where God placed the first man and woman and from where all life flourished. You don't have to believe in my God, or any type of religion, to believe life started somewhere on this planet. Now we can focus on our journey back in time, before we had written history to connect what is happening around the world today. These areas of interest are more than sideshows for tourists, they amplify a profound mystery we need to piece together. By overlooking certain words in Genesis, by not seriously considering the stories told by other religions, and by accepting the denials of science, we've lost sight of other possibilities. Yet one of the greatest treasures lost by man, the Garden of Eden, is one step closer to being uncovered.

Don't continue to read if you're scared of the truth. Before you can see the universe, you have to open your mind to the world in front of you.

CHAPTER IV

A Secret Garden

"The Earth is the cradle of humanity,
but mankind cannot stay in the cradle forever."
—*Konstantin Tsiolkovsky*

I AM CONVINCED THAT the maps we have been discussing are showing us the path back to where man first began, in the Garden of Eden. Therefore, the overlapping points are obviously heavily concentrated on the North American continent rather than in the Middle East, making our story far different from the conventional wisdom and more difficult to prove. Before we begin our voyage into a pollution-free past, to a garden where God(s) placed man, we need to decide whether there was a such place like Eden.

To discover our original ancestral birthplace, we must sift through information left behind by different cultures to try to make sense of what they can teach us about where we came from. Then, we take into account those ancient tales of a Cradle of Life or a Garden of Eden, lay them next to the mysterious locations we have connected in the previous chapter, and see what has been hiding in plain sight.

This would be simple, except that a small problem arises when we discuss what should be accepted as real and what should be considered apocrypha. Our world is plagued with so many versions of our creation that we cannot agree on the same God(s), the same point of origin, or even the same way to exist together. According to estimates, there are more than 4,200 religions or spiritual beliefs around the world, which makes it difficult to cover everyone's faith in this book. Therefore, we'll only consider a handful from different corners of the world, in hopes of finding commonalities with the Christian version of Eden.

Why do I insist on comparing what we find to the Christian version? This is how I was raised, this is how I believe, and this is how I found a path to connection. Since the Bible served as my original point of reference, I use it to connect the dots from there, but to be thorough we will need to open the books of other religions and begin our search.

To start, the beautiful Chinese culture basically has three types of religions and doesn't adhere to one system of faith. Their evolution of beliefs has changed over the years to fit their moral choices and the dictates of their government. But their various versions of mythology have in common the Chinese Daoism legends, an anthology of beliefs that were collected around the first century B.C., telling the tale of the first being, P'an Gu (also written as P'an Ku or Pangu). This God, known to be a hairy being with horns, grew inside a cosmic egg almost 18,000 years ago. He was inside the egg until he was large enough to be

Depiction of P'an Gu

separated from the shell. Afterwards, P'an Gu used the shell to create the separation of wet and dry, night and day, yin and yang, and so on. He sculpted the mountains after he chiseled the valleys. The remnant of pure elements lifted upwards to create the Heavens, while the impure settled to the Earth.

In regions of southern China are people who believe that the universe is the result of P'an Gu's dead body. His eyes became the sun and moon, his blood and sweat became the rivers, trees were formed by his hair, and men were the parasites of P'an Gu's decomposing body.

In other areas of China, some say mankind came from a goddess, Nuwa, or Nu Wa. She is found throughout their legends as a creator, sister, leader, and other roles, including a part in the story of China's Great Deluge. Regarding creation, Nuwa sat alone by a pond one day noticing her reflection, and it was then that the goddess decided to create mankind to keep her company.

Interesting? Definitely. These legends are very poetic and full of unique perspectives. Though we can probably rule out P'an Gu's body as the cause of our cosmic creation, it's fascinating to see the parameters of Chinese beliefs back then. The universe was what they could see on their horizon and did not extend past our galaxy's belt.

Regardless of what you believe, this faith speaks of a beginning firmament, or separation, and the creation of man from a particle source generated by a higher being, all very similar to the order of events that the Bible describes.

As far as complex creation beliefs go, we should begin with the creation stories of the Japanese culture. The country is made up of three main religions, Shinto, Buddhism, and Confucianism, making this a difficult area to research. So many viewpoints explaining where the Japanese came from makes it a hard line to follow. However, I will try to explain it as simply as I can.

Though modern versions have shifted since the 1950s, much of their creation beliefs were written in the eighth century as historical chronicles and taught much like other polytheistic religions. A long list of various deities completes their wide range of mythology, like the Romans and Greeks, with many deities that control particular sections making up the complete world. It is taught that before the Earth existed everything was in unimaginable chaos and without form. Then something transparent and light arose to separate a heaven and materialize a deity called Ame-no-Minaka-Nushi-no-Mikoto. As the opaque and heavy materials in the void began to gather and form the Earth, the Heavens gave birth to Takami-Musubi-no-Mikoto and Kammi-Musubi-no-Mikoto, two more deities.

It's further explained that for millions of years Earth wasn't stable, solid ground. Instead, it was as if the earthly ground floated like oil on the waters. More deities were born out of the Earth during this time, but because it was still in a state of chaos and without real form, the gods and their deity offspring had nothing to do. They called to their two divine beings, Izanagi and Izanami. From there the tale goes into great detail about how these two beings stood on a heavenly bridge and looked at the murky fog of Earth, touched it with a spear adorned with gems, and created the first island, Onokoro. This could be viewed as the Japanese Eden.

Izanagi and Izanami

From there, the story tells of the sun goddess Amaterasu, who sent her grandson Ninigi to one of the Japanese islands to wed one of the earthly deities. Then, in 600 B.C., Ninigi's great-grandson became Japan's first emperor by using a bird that possessed the power to render his enemies helpless.

This creation myth imagines an earth without form that became organized by movements of light matter. It eventually separated into particles of light, or the Heavens, and dark dense particles of mass, which became Earth. This is not too far from the notion of the Big Bang or even the creation firmaments in Genesis. This system is a sort of common ground between religion and science.

Like every religion, there are holes, but the common ground links it to what we have learned from other faiths and from science. It's not a surprise that Christianity is starting to make itself known in Japan with some similar understandings.

Other creation stories from the ancient world have a parallel theme, where a Supreme Being creates mankind from dust, mud, clay, or some kind of particle to serve out a purpose. These stories also include similarities to the Great Flood and the Tower of Babel, which we will discuss in the next chapters. These overlaps carried across a world that supposedly lacked ties.

One of the many things I have come to understand throughout my years of seeking is that the hatred between Christians, Jews, and Muslims is a great paradox. My research made me realize the pointlessness of such hatred, because they all believe in the same God and study the same creation story; it's the perspective that is different.

The Quran 2:87 says, "We gave Moses the Book and followed him up with a succession of Apostles," and Quran 6:91 describes the Book given to Moses as "a light and guidance to man ..." This is the same Moses of the Jews and Christians.

All three faiths speak of the original man and woman in the garden and the tree that later plays a part in the fall of man. While the Muslims use the Quran instead of Genesis, their faith does speak vaguely on the same subject. In Islam, Eden is referred to as "the

Garden," and Adam is created from clay. The Quran gives the first woman the name Hawwa, and she was made out of Adam; it doesn't specify a rib, as does Genesis. Both Adam and Hawwa lived in the garden of paradise, enjoying the blessing of Allah, and were allowed to eat freely of all the garden except one tree. Islam also speaks of Shaytaan, the one who wouldn't bow to Adam, as the enemy of man who would use deception to try to drive them out.

This sounds familiar to my own understanding of the Creation and the Fall of man. Finding common ground among humans will never be easy, and reaching agreement that we all come from the same source is even harder. If we can start from the beginning, Eden, or the garden, and branch out from there, we may find that we are all standing closer together than we thought. However, using only scriptural guides may not be the way to get the answers we need.

I do not propose that our scriptures don't hold the keys to the answers we seek, because they do, and I do not imply that there isn't truth to be found inside the pages of our scriptural history. But we are tasked with sorting truth from personally structured doctrines redesigned to rule the people. Much like the other doctrines of faith, Genesis gives us a starting point regarding where God(s) placed us on Earth, inside the beautiful walls of the Garden of Eden. A place where a river flowed out of her gates and separated into four rivers towards the world, where the first man and woman, Adam and Eve, lived peacefully with their family and all the beasts. A place from which they were later banished, not only from its doors but also from the presence of the God(s) that put them there.

Will any of this prove there is a such a place as the Garden of Eden? No. But it shows that many people from across our globe, not just Christians, believe that man was created on Earth, or from the Earth, and spread out from that point—basically a cradle of life.

Eden is one of the many locations that archeologists would like to find. Is it possible that Eden is somewhere other than where scholars have speculated and where archeologists have been looking? Yes. Could it have been in North America? Yes, again. What clues match up with where our maps led us in previous chapters? Archeology has taught us many facts about prehistoric cultures that have been lost over the years, but now we can look through what they've found for clues to lead us closer to Eden.

Let us begin with the Sumerians, the first civilization in southern Mesopotamia, which is thought to be the birthplace of the Garden of Eden stories. Although they're not the oldest civilization, their texts use some of the earliest written languages found so far. Their culture left behind writings that span 3500-3000 B.C. and preceded the Babylonians, who were once thought to be the oldest civilization.

In the 19th century, in the valleys of the Tigris and Euphrates in modern day Iraq, archaeologists unearthed the remains of cities where the Sumerians had once flourished. The remains of their texts carry some of the earliest literary works displaying epic tales, including man's creation, a warning of an imminent flood, and plenty of confusing names for the gods. Does any of this sound familiar? Indeed it does. Stories crossing over from religion to religion has been the theme.

The problem with the notion of Mesopotamia being Eden is in the details. If you follow the clues, Eden is not likely to have existed in this location. The following map shows the theoretical location of Mesopotamia, where the Sumerian civilization and the Garden of Eden are believed to be, according to most archaeologists.

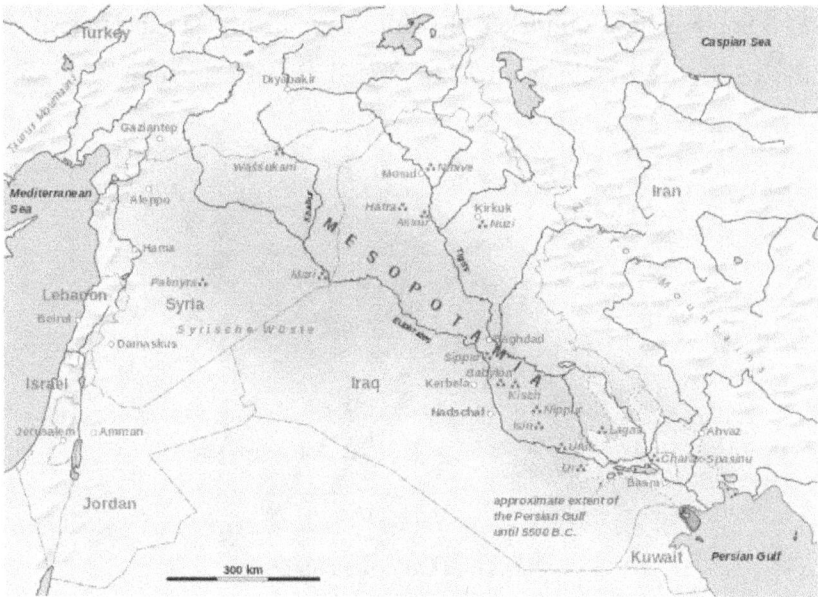

Mesopotamia

Using both Biblical scriptures and Sumerian text, we know that there were rivers mentioned outside of the garden. Genesis 2:10 gives the direction that a river went out of Eden and split into four river heads. The following image shows that in the land of Sumer, only one of the four rivers mentioned in Genesis exists, the Euphrates.

Euphrates River

Some believe Hiddekel, the third river mentioned in Genesis, is the Tigris, because the word is interpreted to mean "the rapid Tigris."

Tigris and Euphrates Rivers

These seem to line up, except the Tigris and the Euphrates flow in the wrong direction. In order to find Eden, these rivers need to have a main river to source the water from which they flow, and not flow into the Persian Gulf near Mesopotamia.

GENESIS 2:10

¹⁰ And a river went out of Eden to water the garden;
and from thence it was parted, and became into four heads.

Since these two rivers flow toward Sumer, the archaeological theory is flawed. To further dispel this theory, where are the other two rivers, the Pison and the Gihon, that are mentioned in Genesis 2:11-13? There isn't much to go on because they don't appear on any maps, and no major rivers are close enough to the Tigris and Euphrates.

This doesn't mean that we've reached a dead end. It simply means that archaeologists have been looking in the wrong place. Earth has been reshaped over its lifetime, since the age of Pangea as well as after the Great Flood. Let's do a little archaeological work ourselves. Look at the next map. Where do the Tigris and Euphrates flow on the map of Pangea?

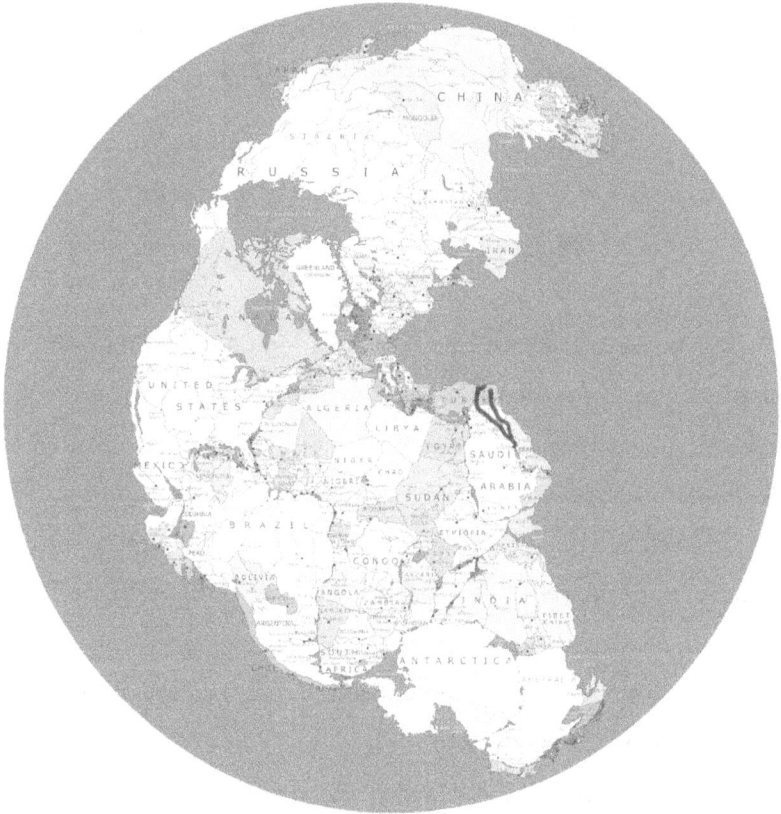

The Tigris and Euphrates on Pangea

Unless the Garden of Eden was located in the middle of the ocean, the two rivers don't appear to be connected to a main water source with land, as mentioned in Genesis 2:11-14.

GENESIS 2:11 – 14

¹¹ The name of the first is Pison: that is it which compasseth the whole land of Havilah, where there is gold;

¹² And the gold of that land is good: there is bdellium and the onyx stone.

¹³ And the name of the second river is Gihon: the same is it that compasseth the whole land of Ethiopia.

¹⁴ And the name of the third river is Hiddekel: that is it which goeth toward the east of Assyria. And the fourth river is Euphrates.

These passages tell us we are looking for a total of four rivers that were once part of a great river. Let us pause for a minute to look at what the passages say, and visit who actually wrote these passages to discover more about where these rivers might be located.

It's believed that Genesis was given to us by Moses, which is probably true. Even the Quran speaks of Moses being given the Books. However, he may have been more of the finishing writer who compiles years of ancestral writing into one book, rather than the actual author of each chapter. Let me explain.

Many scholars have noted that the way Genesis is written isn't uniform. The language in Genesis is different, the name of God is used differently, and hints of Egyptian phrases are also used, as if multiple people gave their accounts with journals over the years and handed them down to later be pieced together by Moses.

In the 1930s, a man by the name P.J. Wiseman, who spent a lot of time near archeological sites in the Middle East, noticed a common theme in the way ancient tablets ended. When a writer of a tablet was finished, he would sign it with *"this is a written history/genealogy of…"* or *"this is the year of…"* and even sign his name. Wiseman observed that these types of statements also happened several times in Genesis. The following are the scriptures that theoretically break up the different writers of Genesis:

2:4   *These are the generations of the heavens and of the earth when they were created, in the day that the LORD God made the earth and the heavens,*

5:1   *This is the book of the generations of Adam, In the day that God created man, in the likeness of God made he him*

6:9   *These are the generations of Noah: Noah was a just man and perfect in his generations, and Noah walked with God.*

10:1 *Now these are the generations of the sons of Noah, Shem, Ham, and Japheth: and unto them were sons born after the flood.*

11:10 *These are the generations of Shem: Shem was an hundred years old, and begat Arphaxad two years after the flood*

11:27 *Now these are the generations of Terah: Terah begat Abram, Nahor, and Haran; and Haran begat Lot*

25:19 *And these are the generations of Isaac, Abraham's son: Abraham begat Isaac:*

> *37:2 These are the generations of Jacob. Joseph, being*
> *seventeen years old, was feeding the flock with his*
> *brethren;*

Why is this important? If we think that Genesis is a linear story told by one man who never witnessed the events, it loses its historical value for many. But if, when he became the leader of Israel, he was handed the history of the Lord's people to later edit into one book, then it would make more sense and hold more weight as historical truth. In addition, it would help us understand why there is a dead end when we look for Eden. If Moses wrote it from the beginning, he would know the location of Eden, and he might have given extra reference to the places mentioned that no longer appear on the map of Moses' day.

The only river name we recognize is the Euphrates, therefore we immediately assume Eden would be somewhere near Mesopotamia. However, if Adam was the author of the first segment that was later handed to Noah and taken onto the Ark and then handed all the way down to Moses, it changes perspective and opens the possibility that Eden was somewhere other than Mesopotamia.

Also, if the beginning part was written before the Flood, Adam wouldn't have seen the modern Euphrates. It would make sense that the rivers of Sumer in Mesopotamia were named after the Flood occurred. It would not be unusual for the rivers found near where the Ark landed to have names similar to those mentioned by their ancestors, which might also explain why only two of the four are found.

Throughout history, pioneers often named newly explored areas after ones they knew. Even street names tend to be repetitive.

Let's return to trying to find the four rivers mentioned in Genesis.

First, use the next map to examine the globe's major rivers and consider where they might have been in the beginning.

Major river systems in the world

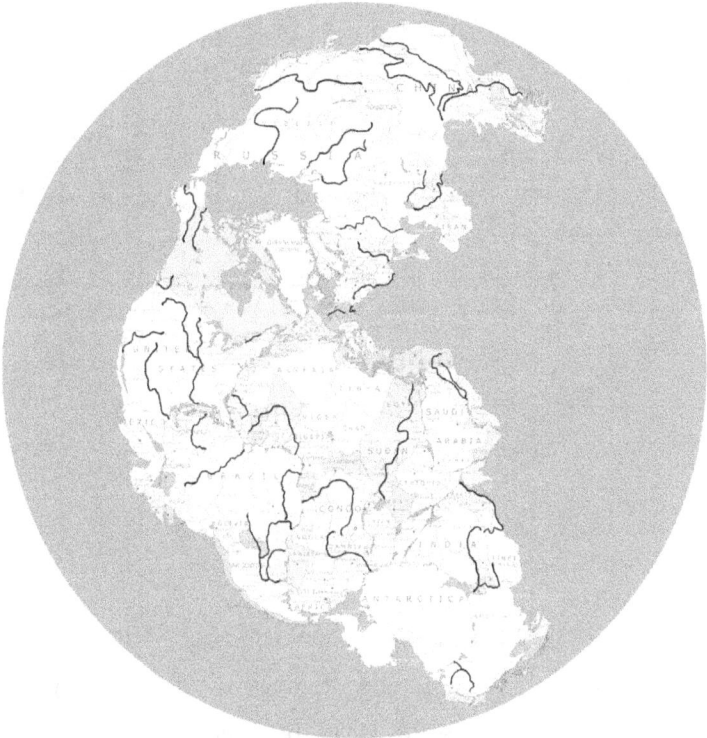

Major river systems located on Pangea

These main river systems at first appear to be sourced from the oceans or to flow into the ocean, but when we mark them on Pangea, they appear to be shooting off randomly from within the large land mass. The following map adds a theoretical outline of waterways that these main rivers could've connected to and smaller rivers that have branched off inland, making it all connect.

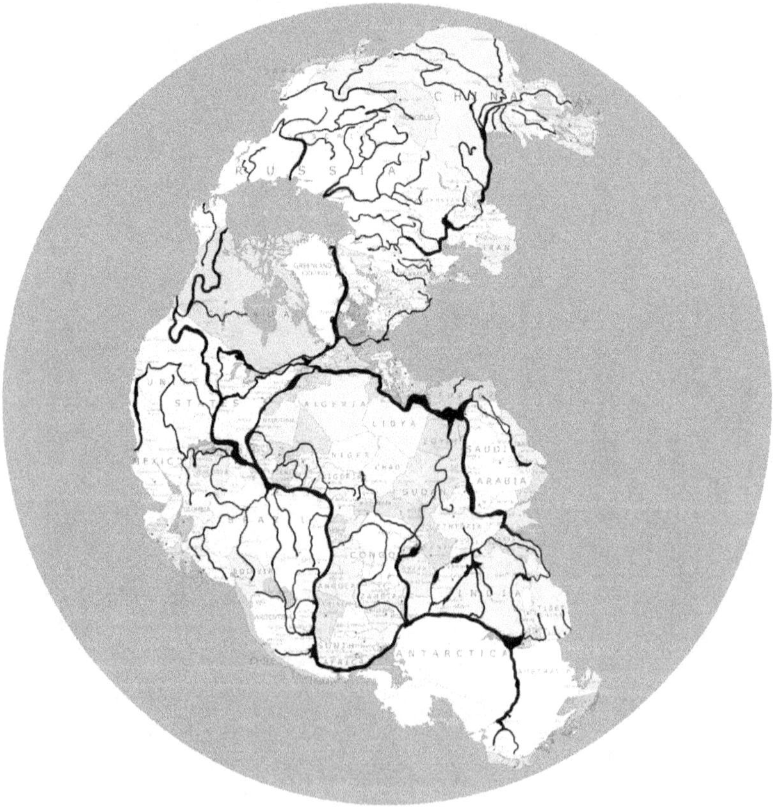

Theoretical river channels

With this possible river connection, let's see how this ties into the rivers mentioned in Genesis. Try to trace them back to the gates, where a single river went out of Eden. In Genesis 2:10-14, we can get clues about the rivers that went out of Eden to water the garden.

GENESIS 12:10 – 14

¹⁰ And a river went out of Eden to water the garden; and from thence it was parted, and became into four heads.

¹¹ The name of the first is Pison: that is it which compasseth the whole land of Havilah, where there is gold;

¹² And the gold of that land is good: there is bdellium and the onyx stone.

¹³ And the name of the second river is Gihon: the same is it that compasseth the whole land of Ethiopia.

¹⁴ And the name of the third river is Hiddekel: that is it which goeth toward the east of Assyria. And the fourth river is Euphrates.

It's suggested that the Pison is large enough to wrap a large area of land rich in gold as well as bdellium and onyx. We know about gold and onyx; it's speculated that bdellium refers to precious stones, crystals, or even pearls, but it's not certain. Equally, the location of the land of Havilah is in question. Though Havilah is mentioned later in the Bible as a name and also again as a place, it is after the Flood and could very well be a place named after the stories from Eden. The next maps show where the Pison would be located on Pangea and how those same areas are known for an abundance of gold.

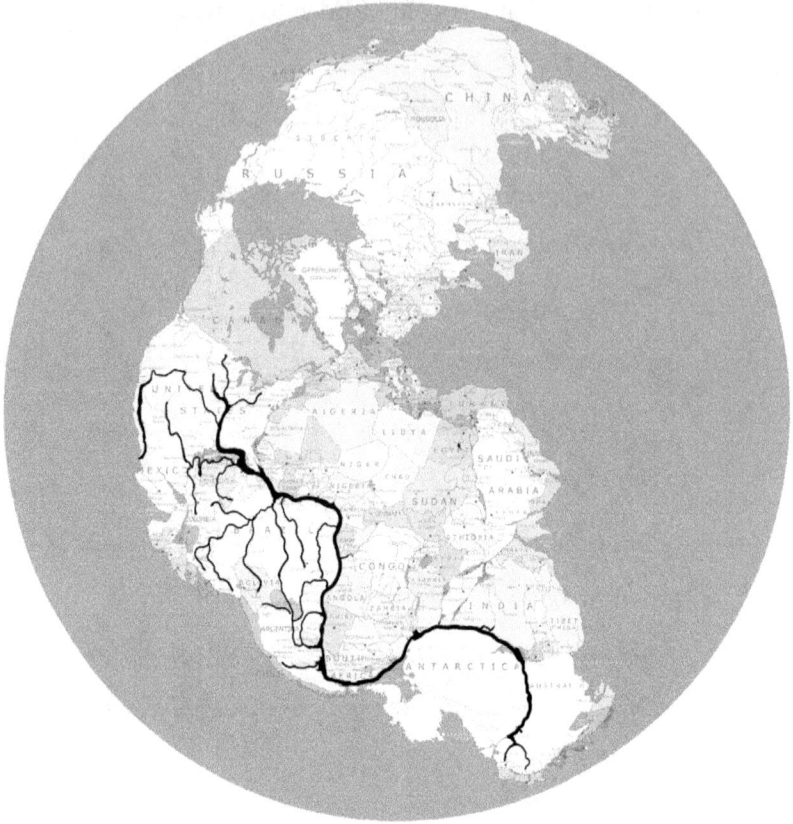

Pison on Pangea

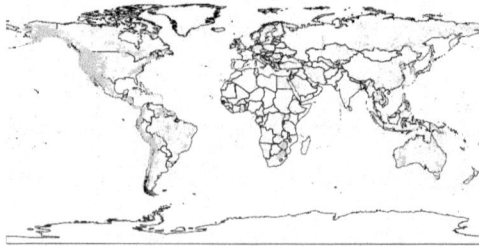

Map of global gold mining

The second river mentioned, the Gihon, also a large river, was said to encompass the whole land of Ethiopia. Historically we know that Ethiopia doesn't have the same borders today as it did when it was first colonized. Neither was it the same land spoken of when Genesis was written. Most generally, when Ethiopia is mentioned in the Bible, it's referring to all the land south of Egypt, which lends credence to the argument that the river outline on Pangea is the Gihon.

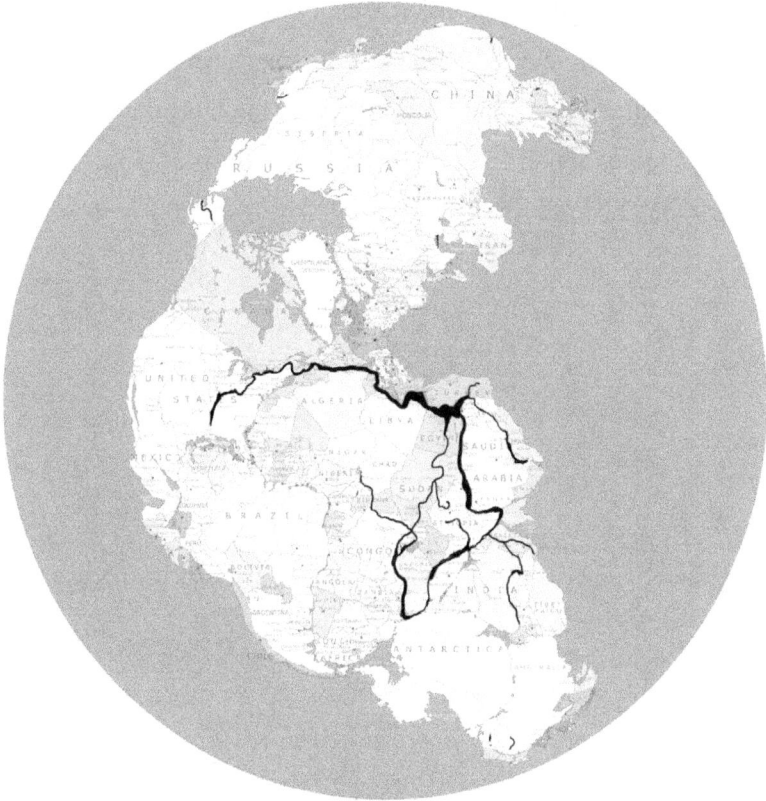

Gihon River

Now to the third river, the one thought to be the modern-day Tigris, the Hiddekel in v.14. Since we are presuming this was information given to us by Adam directly, we can assume that this river went east past the Assyria of Adam's day. If it was Assyria in the late 14th century, the description "... *the third river is Hiddekel: that is it which goeth toward the east of Assyria"* wouldn't be the Tigris most assume today to be the Hiddekel. Until 600 B.C., the Assyrian Empire was a large area located around present-day Iraq and Syria, and the Tigris was one of its main rivers. It does not fit the parameters of Genesis 2:14.

In a later chapter I will present the science behind the shifting magnetic north, and discuss the possibility that at the time of Eden it was centralized in North America. For now, understand that north would be centralized around the Midwest of the United States. Which also lends more support to the theory that Eden was in North America, and that the Hiddekel River went east, as shown on the next map.

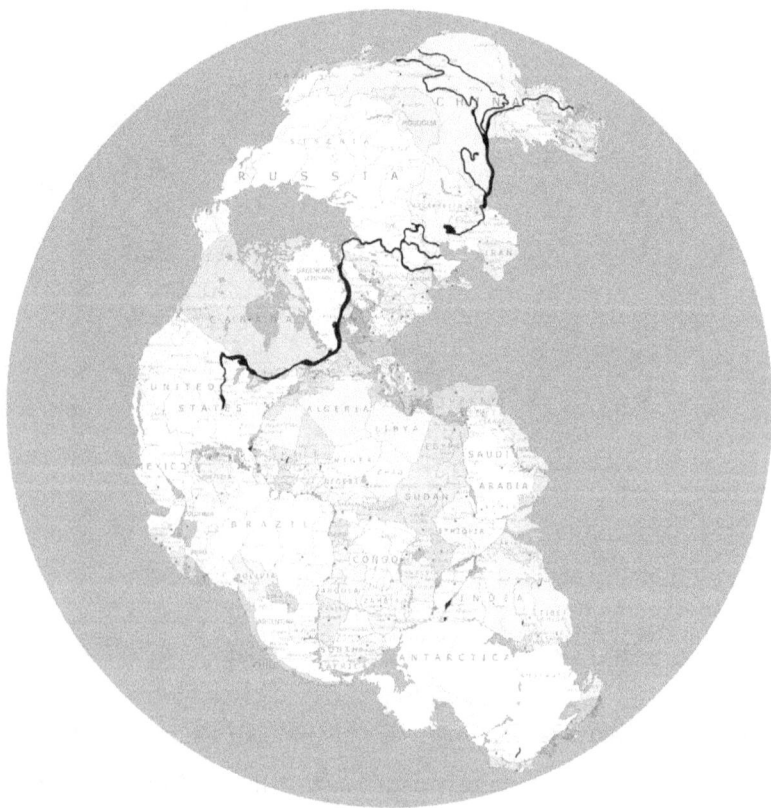

Hiddekel River

This leaves us with the last-mentioned river, the Euphrates. There are no other clues about it during the time of Eden, except that it is the fourth river. The Hiddekel and the Euphrates both flow east on Pangea, so without more information, it's possible that these could be flip-flopped.

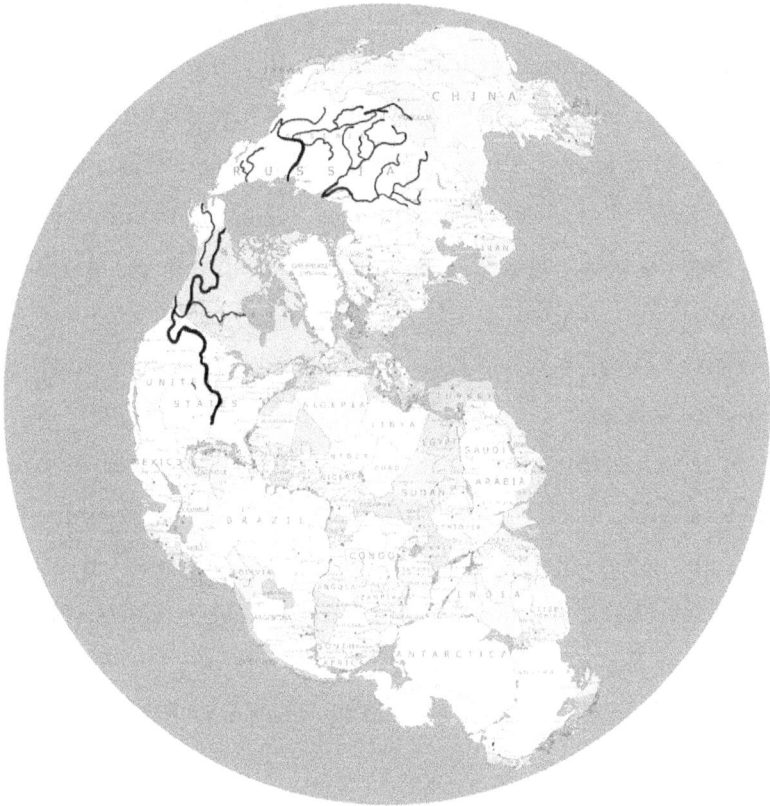

Euphrates River

The first mention of the Euphrates is in Genesis 2:14, but the writer didn't describe it fully. In Genesis 15:18, when it's mentioned with the covenant between God and Abraham, the Euphrates is referred to as the great river. Later, it seems to be used as a major reference point for the boundaries of the northeast kingdom. The Euphrates is one of the more important rivers in western Asia and one of the largest, spanning about 1,700 miles. The fact that it's mentioned first in regard to being one of the rivers out of Eden supports my hypothesis that today's Euphrates is not the original one. It only became the great river after the Flood; one of the sources that feed the Euphrates is the Murat river, which is near Ararat.

It is not blasphemy to believe that God(s) created this vast planet and that a great multitude of Biblical events happened in areas other than the Middle East. We've only been led to believe this is the truth, having received our history over the ages by word of mouth, then into text that has been changed and diluted time and time again. It's also not wrong to think that if a God was going to banish man from the Garden of Eden, he would do so by sending him toward another land separated by a great distance, like the Middle East.

I've staked my claim that I believe Eden is located in North America, and I'm not the only one who believes this. Regarding the maps, this information is all new and has not been connected to Eden prior to this book. But there is a religion that believes in what Genesis teaches but also teaches about groups of people who also lived in the Americas. That religion believes that the Garden of Eden is in North America.

The Church of Jesus Christ of Latter-day Saints doesn't have doctrine on Eden's exact location, but the church owns a large area of land located in Daviess County, Missouri, that it believes is the sacred ground where Adam and Eve lived after being expelled from Eden.

Missouri, located in the United States

Adam-ondi-Ahman stones

In 1838, the stones located on this site were proclaimed to be a part of the altar on which Adam offered up sacrifices to Jehovah, and this was the valley of God in which Adam blessed his children. This area plays perfectly into the map showing where the rivers point on Pangea.

It's evident as well that God loves all his people and has revealed things to many, not just those of one faith. Taking into account all the overlapping stories, the unexplained pathways of the paranormal, and the matching up of rivers, it's possible to believe that this location or another in America could be important to the history of God's creation.

When the Garden of Eden is mentioned, we automatically think of the Middle East, but if it was located in the middle of North America near the Mississippi River, this would throw off the whole first part of Genesis. It would also mean there are more places we could be looking for in the wrong direction, and it would suggest that Noah left in the ark somewhere around Missouri. How crazy would it be if we could find clues to link the idea that Noah was also in America at one point before the flood and confirm that Eden was also there? Keep reading.

CHAPTER V

The Great Flood

"Heavy hearts, like heavy clouds in the sky, are
best relieved by the letting of a little water."
—*Christopher Morley*

THE GREAT FLOOD is one of the more talked-about events throughout most religions, but did it really happen? Of course it did. We just cannot agree on how much of the Earth was actually flooded or how many people were spared.

Today, many scientists can show us proof that some type of flooding, or possibly multiple floods, happened across the globe thousands of years ago. The debate is fueled when minor details are discredited and people who believe in the validity of The Great Flood feel that their beliefs—including belief in the everlasting power of their God(s)—are being challenged.

For example, many have bickered over the detail of the rainbow appearing to signify the end of the Flood. Does the existence of God really depend on whether or not there was a rainbow in the story? No, it doesn't. But common sense suggests that the amount of water that fell, as portrayed by the various flood myths, would've created a rainbow that the survivors would have seen, whether or not only a few major areas were covered or the whole planet was engulfed.

There are over 200 versions of flood stories spread throughout history. We can't say for certain how accurate each fable is. But we can pull out the overlapping points and compare them side by side to create something closer to evidence, just as we did with Eden. This book won't cover all versions, but we will touch on a few flood myths that have parallels.

When breaking down these stories from different religions, keep in mind that we have written scriptures to jog memories and serve as references, whereas the ancients had to remember stories that were passed to them from their elders by word of mouth.

Regardless, these stories about creation and the Flood, though slightly altered down through the generations, hold much weight because of the repeated themes. The fact that similar stories have found their way into countless religions is more evidence of their worth and should be taken into consideration.

On a side note, some of the landmarks will be based on current locations when referencing landing sites. As previously discussed, Genesis 10 mentions the land separating, which gives us insight into an era when the land began dividing. Since not all the facts are available, science can only guess that it took millions of years for the Pangea landmass to separate. However, the details in Genesis open up the possibility that it happened not that long ago.

GENESIS 7:11 – 12

11 In the six hundredth year of Noah's life, in the second month, the seventeenth day of the month, the same day were all the fountains of the great deep broken up, and the windows of heaven were opened.

[12] And the rain was upon the earth forty days and forty nights.

GENESIS 8:2

[2] The fountains also of the deep and the windows of heaven were stopped, and the rain from heaven was restrained;

These verses tell us that for 40 days and 40 nights not only did it rain, but there were also constant earthquakes. These earthquakes definitely started the process of moving the continents closer to where they are today. With unrelieved continental disruption, it's possible to change the face of the Earth over the whole year that Noah spent on the Ark.

Now, before we get too carried away with only mentioning Noah, let's recount some of the other stories of the Flood. First, let us compare the Genesis version alongside the Sumerian version found in the Epic of Gilgamesh. Both share a story of a great flood that is to come to Earth because the God(s) had decided to wipe out mankind. In Genesis, we are told that it was because of man's wickedness that the Earth would flood, whereas in the Sumerian account, man had become too noisy for the Gods' tolerance. These stories both echo the theme of a male hero to survive the rising waters, Noah (Genesis) and Utnapishtim (Epic of Gilgamesh), each guided by one of their Gods to build a boat strong enough to hold their families and a multitude of animals before the deity-directed genocide began.

Interestingly, the Sumerian flood gives only six or seven days and nights of rain, which indirectly suggests a local event since there wouldn't be enough rainfall to cover the Earth in such a short time. We are told in Genesis that the rains came 40 days and 40 nights along with springs from below to assist in creating a global flood.

A common element in these two accounts is how these two different men learned it was safe to leave their boats. Both sent three birds to find out if the waters were low enough to proceed with the rebirth of life. This implies that the God(s) of these men gave them instructions to bring enough birds along.

These versions differ in some minor details, but it's fascinating how their main points agree. Consider, for example, that the boats in these two stories supposedly ended up on mountain ranges only 300 miles apart. Genesis tells us that Noah landed on the mountains of Ararat. In the Epic of Gilgamesh, Utnapishtim landed on Nisir.

Arguments over which of these stories came first have been ongoing since the tablets of the Epic of Gilgamesh were discovered in the mid-nineteenth century near Mesopotamia. Some proclaim that the elders of the Jewish faith have kept excellent oral records of creation throughout history that predate those findings. Additionally, we went over the possibility that Genesis was written from a first account and handed down to Moses, which would also mean that Noah took the records with him. We still don't know who is telling the real story.

Another account of a flood that incorporates many Gods, like the Sumerian text, is that of the Greeks, which yields three different flood stories. In one version, we have Prometheus, the God best known for his creation of man. Prometheus was in conflict with Zeus, the God of the sky and the ruler over the Gods of Olympus. Zeus was tired of the disobedient and greedy ways of mankind and decided to destroy them. In an effort to save the people of earth, the son of Prometheus begged Zeus to be merciful, but Zeus had already decided to end man.

Prometheus told his son to build an ark to withstand the flood, much like Noah and Utnapishtim. In the Greek stories, the rains lasted only nine days and nights before the rising waters ceased. Interestingly, in this story, survivors included not only those on the ark but also the people who ran to the top of mountains, who also escaped the genocide. Afterwards, the son of Prometheus and his wife landed atop a mountain, believed to be Parnassus, and offered a sacrifice. There is definitely a common theme with boats, a selected man and his kin, and landing upon a mountain of sorts.

Our next flood story also has a similar theme. A Great Flood is mentioned twice in the Islamic writings of the Quran, both in Sura 11 and Sura 71, and sheds light on how familiar Christianity is to its proclaimed enemy. If you're unfamiliar with the Quran's teachings and prophets, note that this version's hero is also Noah, and we are told the story through the words of Allah, which is God.

In Sura 11:40 and Sura 11:44, the fountains of the earth opened to aid the rising waters coming from the rains, as in the Genesis account. However, here Noah and his family may not have been the only ones willing to heed the warning:

SURA 11:40

"At length, behold! There came Our Command, and the fountains of the earth gushed forth! We said: 'Embark therein, of each two, male and female, and your family— except those against whom the Word has already gone forth,—and the believers.' But only a few believed with him."

SURA 11:44

"Then the word went forth: 'O earth! Swallow up thy water, and O sky! withhold (thy rain)! And the water abated, and the matter was ended. The Ark rested on Mount Judi, and the word went forth: 'Away with those who do wrong!' "

These passages from the Quran share the Islamic recordings of Noah and those near to him, making it easy to teach that it could've been a localized flood. But the statement that "the fountains of the

Earth gushed forth" leaves room to believe the flood in this version could have been a worldwide event, as Genesis teaches. We are also led to believe that a few other faithful people might have survived the devastation to aid in the repopulation of the world, which the Greek and Sumerian stories also teach.

Genesis 8:4 says the ark rested "upon the mountains" of Ararat and the people on board offered a sacrifice and then settled east of the mountains. The Quran states the ark rested on Mount Judi, southwest of Ararat, and those aboard also offered a sacrifice. Mount Judi on a map is also known as Mount Cudi due to cultural pronunciation. The following shows its proximity to Ararat.

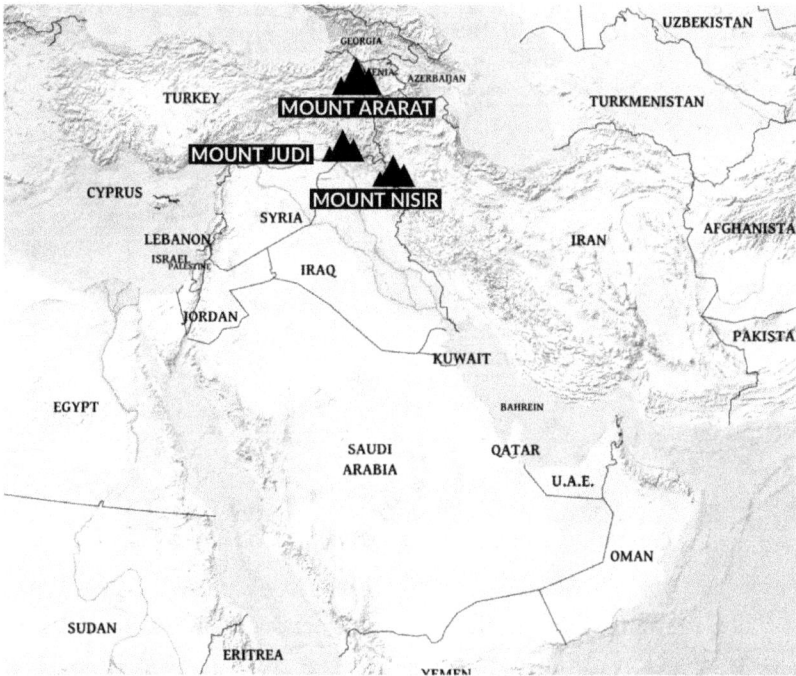

Some believe the tomb of Noah is near these Ark resting places. It would be nice if we could prove that one of these sites held the remains of a man whose DNA allowed mankind to hit restart.

The Greeks point to Parnassus, in the southern part of Greece, as the landing spot for their hero. Could there be a connection to these places? If we erase the lines representing the borders of countries and look at "the mountains" of Ararat before territories were established, the mountain range spans a much larger area. The next map gives the locations of the mountaintops where different religions claim their arks landed.

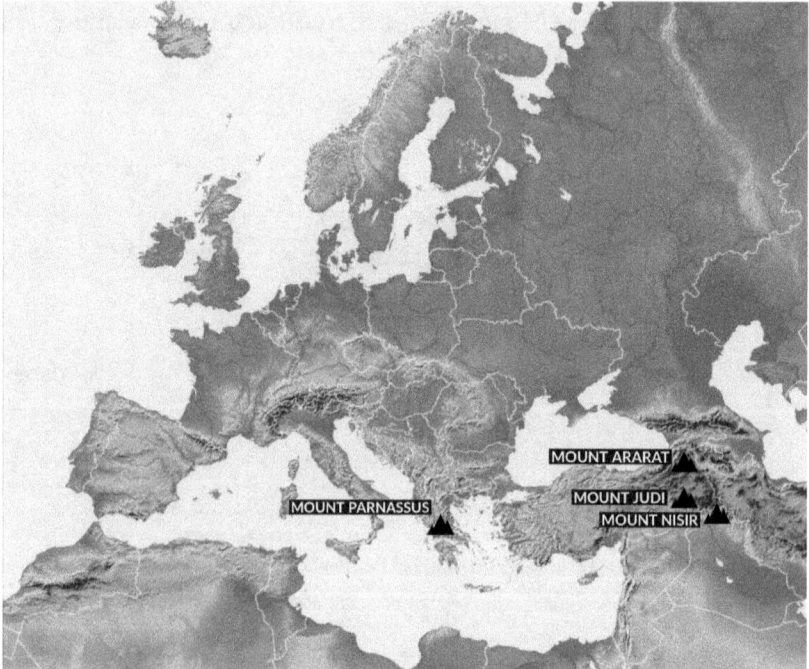

Correlating stopping points of multiple landing points

To present one more flood story and show additional correlation, let's look to the mythology of the Hindu people, which tells of a man called Manu, who was created by the gods to be the first king of Earth. One of the greatest stories told about him is of the great flood that destroyed everything on Earth.

Manu found a tiny fish in a bowl of water one day. The fish offered a trade. He said that if Manu would place him in something bigger, in hopes of surviving, he would save Manu from the flood that was coming. Manu agreed and continued to place the fish into bigger and bigger tanks until eventually he threw him into the sea. At that point, the fish warned Manu that he should build a large ship to save himself and that it needed to be able to carry two of each animal and the seeds of each kind of plant. Manu built the ship and tied it to the horn growing out of the fish, awaiting the flooding water. As the waters rose, the fish pulled Manu through to the Himalayan mountains where he told him to wait for the land to dry. Manu was lonely since he was the only survivor, so he offered sacrifice and was given a wife to repopulate the earth.

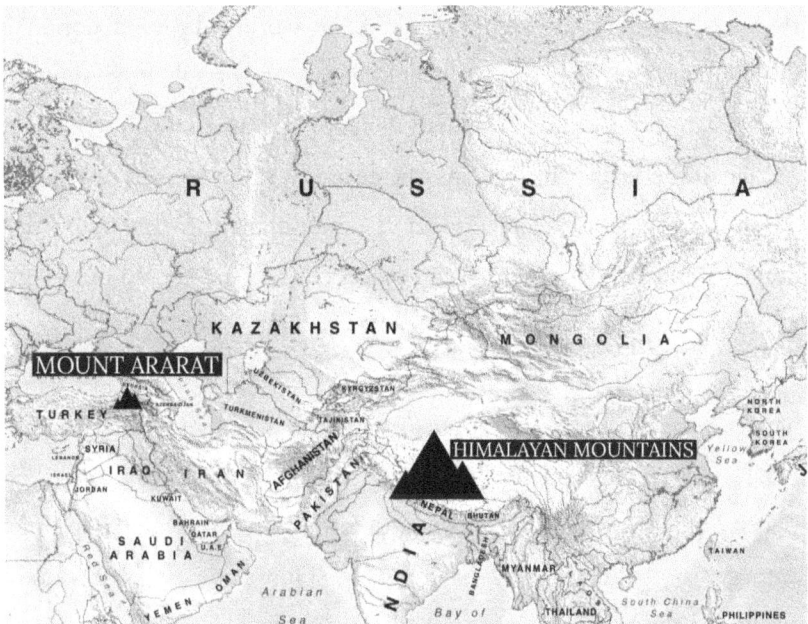

So was this a local event? Probably not; or at least it wasn't only in one location. Again, common sense tells us a lot, even before we look from a different angle. For example, the stories we reviewed about the flood portray the main character, a man, building a large boat because a powerful being told him a massive flood was coming to wipe out mankind. If it was a local event, the God in these stories could have merely told his faithful people to relocate to a place where the water wouldn't rise. Consider Noah, who was given more than a hundred years to prepare.

In addition, we know that an all-powerful God can simply make it rain but didn't. Instead, these men were warned and given ample time to build a huge boat and gather animals of all kinds. Let's not forget that building a boat of that magnitude in the time of these legends would take longer than it would today.

Scholars continue to debate whether the flood was a local event that was exaggerated over time, or if the worldwide flood notion is more likely represented by a combination of several areas showing geological evidence of a massive flood. Because we have barely scratched the surface in studying the entire Earth, who is to say the ark did not settle somewhere else in the mountains of Ararat, or that multiple arks captained by several patriarchs of God settled on several mountain ranges?

To survive, a massive boat carrying animals and people would have to avoid the sharp points of mountain ranges. Therefore, if Noah's Ark landed on the mountains of Ararat, it seems more likely that it landed closer to the shores and lower parts of Ararat to prevent damage to the underbelly of the Ark. This same thought can be applied to the human reset stories of other faiths.

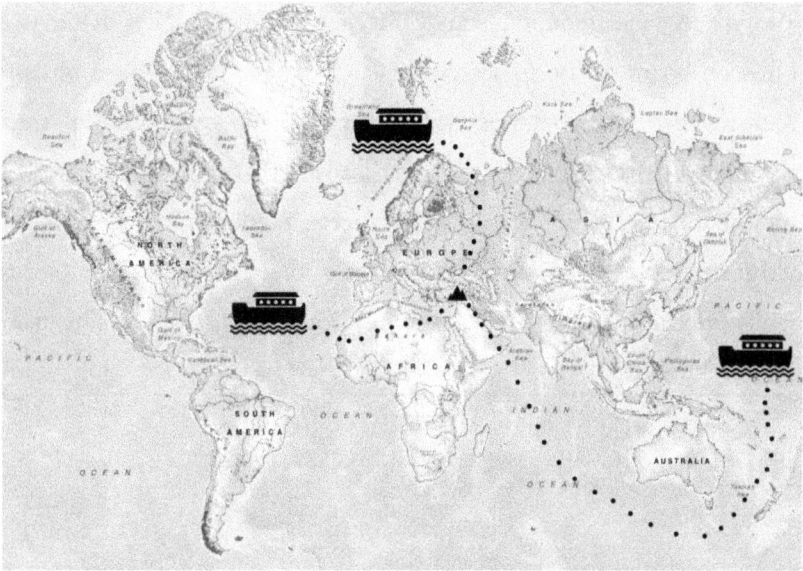

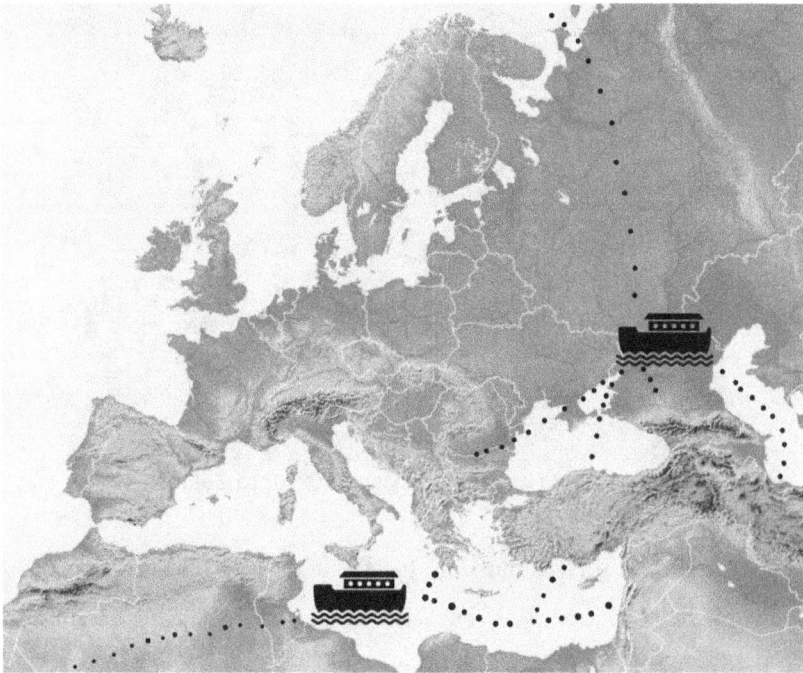

Possible safe routes toward the mountains near Ararat

The routes shown on the map above would also be far enough

away from other mountains and hills, supporting the tales of carrying birds on board to use to search for land. One wouldn't need birds to seek out dry land if it was visible from the top deck. One of these routes overlaps a unique spot in Turkey that's on the side of a mountain. It's an unlikely area to place a random circle of columns weighing several tons, but a perfect spot to set up several temples to make offerings, and it's only 490 miles from Mount Ararat. This place is Göbekli Tepe.

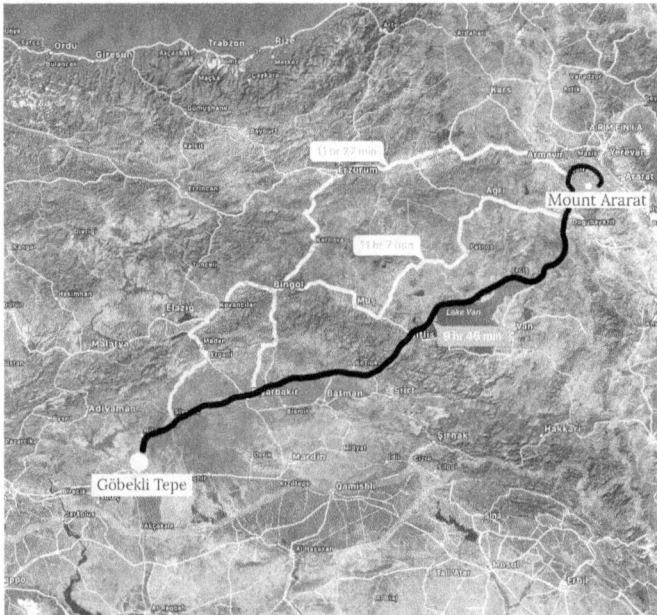

Current driving routes from Mount Ararat to Göbekli Tepe

These next images illustrate the fascination of Göbekli Tepe. Not only is the location ideal, but also notice the beautiful carvings of animals and the use of circular formations.

Göbekli Tepe

As I mentioned, the carvings found on these columns are of many kinds of animals, but some are not indigenous to the area. That fits the ark stories that describe the gathering of animals. Why would anyone build high up in the mountains? Many times in the Bible, men climbed up into the mountains to make offerings to their God. It's also likely the Ark could have landed nearby. It would make sense that if God spared them from the Great Flood, an altar of sacrifice would be placed high on a mountainside with both size and beauty for God to see.

Göbekli Tepe is not only close to the proclaimed landing sites of the Ark (and the alternate Ark pathways) but also to the Tigris and

Euphrates rivers. This reiterates how the people who survived the Flood named the rivers after coming down from the Ark.

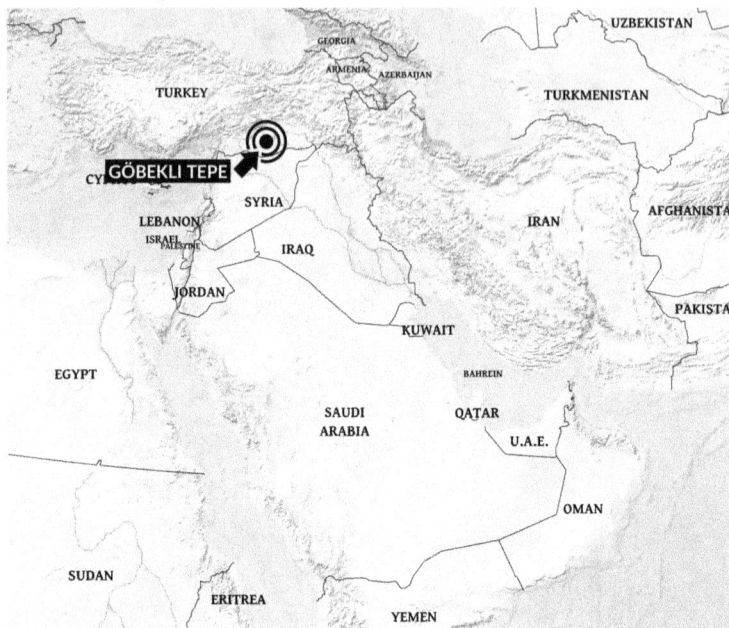

Additional evidence that points to this vicinity being the second birthplace of man is a very old tree. The Olive Tree of Vouves is located on the Greek Island of Crete, which is around 260 miles west of Göbekli Tepe. What is unique about this area is the age of this olive tree and many others that originate in this area. The Olive Tree of Vouves is thought to be anywhere from 3,000 to 5,000 years old.

The significance of the olive tree is found throughout the scriptures in the New Testament, but the first mention is in Genesis 8:11, when the dove returns with an olive leaf in her mouth to let Noah know the water had receded. It's not mentioned again until Exodus. The olive tree wasn't originally found across the globe, but by way of man, it has been transplanted worldwide.

These are all tremendous clues left behind to give us a better idea of where the Ark landed, so now let us look at where Noah might have built the Ark before the flood. We mentioned in the previous chapter that if the Garden of Eden is in North America, and if Adam and Eve lived near the Mississippi River, then Noah would have also lived nearby and possibly built the Ark there.

About a mile from the Mississippi River is a marvelous structure that baffles archeologists, who don't know how or why it was built. In Chapter 2 we discussed a location in Illinois that has a base much like the base of a pyramid. The structure, known as Monks Mound, is in an odd location. Not only was it constructed on a floodplain, but it was built in an area that lacked the materials used to build it. Whoever designed this mound used a rainbow of soils (red, orange, brown, black, blue and grey), limestone slabs, and cypress and red cedar posts.

Those who have researched the area are amazed at how such a mound was constructed. The blue soil alone is very rare; the closest place known to have such soil is in Clay County, Indiana, 180 miles east of the mound. It's estimated that the mound consists of more than 2 billion pounds of soil. Researchers estimate this site would have required more than 15,000 people carrying 50-pound baskets nonstop to provide this amount of soil within a few years.

Originally, archeologists thought Monks Mound was built over the course of 250 years, but after studying the seeds and spores found in the soil they estimate it happened in a fraction of that time. What if you had 60 to 80 years and two oxen to carry cartloads of soil? The following is an equation to simply break down the possibility of Noah and his kin building this site.

Monks Mound Equation

- 2.6 billion pounds or soil, w/ average oxen pulling 1,500-3,000 each, equations based on 2 oxen per cart

@ 3,000 lbs. per trip, w/ 1 ox
       2.16B / 3,000 = 720,000 trips

@ 6,000 lbs. per trip w/ 2 oxen per cart, which is more likely
       2,16B / 6,000 = 360,000 trips

- Noah had 3 sons to help, Noah could help, as well we know Methuselah (Noah's grandfather) died in the year of the Flood and could've helped, Lamech (Noah's father) died 5 years before that and also could've helped.

@ 3,000 lbs, w/5 men helping, w/1 ox cart per person
       720,000 / 5 = 144,000 trips

@ 6,000lbs, w/ 5 men helping, w/ 2 oxen cart per person
       360,000 / 5 = 72,000 trips

- Noah was given 100-120 years warning of the flood, and it is estimated it took 40 years to build the Ark

@ 60 years (100-40)
       144,000 trips / 60yrs = 2,400 trips per year / 313 days (365-52 Sabbath days of not working) = 7.66 trips a day

       72,000 trips / 60yrs = 12,000 trips per yr / 313 days = 3.83 trips per day

@ 80 years (120-40)
       144,000 trips / 80yrs = 1,800 trips per yr / 313 days = 5.75 trips per day

       72,000 trip / 80yrs = 900 trips per yr / 313 days = 2.87 days

The equation is based on five men (Noah's grandfather, Methuselah; Noah's father, Lamech; Noah's three sons; and Noah himself) having large carts to pull the soil. The equation, however, doesn't account for the possibility that Noah may have had other family members alive during the building of the Ark who died before the Flood. Also, Noah might have hired others to help with the project with hopes of bringing them along, especially since there is evidence of a large number of people living near this area. Moreover, the equation doesn't account for different soil weights changing the number of trips each soil individually would take. Noah was given 100-120 years' notice of the coming flood, and not all were spent on the Ark alone. These calculations are purely to show that it could have been accomplished by Noah in the time frame he was given, leaving him 40 years to build the Ark.

When you look at the way Monks Mound is designed, you can easily see how it could have held the Ark and would have been sloped enough for animals to board when it was time. Consider also that erosion has changed the shape over the past several thousand years.

Monks Mound

GENESIS 7:17

¹⁷ And the flood was forty days upon the earth; and the waters increased, and bare up the ark, and it was lift up above the earth.

As the verse in Genesis 7:17 insinuates, the Ark was lifted off the earth by the waters; it wasn't built next to the shoreline and then pushed into the ocean to wait for the Flood. So, if it was built on this particular floodplain in Illinois, the water would have risen around it as it sat on Monks Mound, and the soils brought in from other areas would have held the Ark in place until it was time to set sail.

What does archeology tell us about the Flood? For starters, the world was moderately populated during the pre-Flood era, with probably millions of people spread across the face of the earth. We have evidence across the globe that some type of flood happened thousands of years ago. There is proof that the planet was also covered with a lot of glacial ice, which means there was a lot less ocean covering the land. Our favorite beach destinations were actually inland cities.

For example, until about 7,000 years ago (about 5,000 B.C.), the Black Sea was a body of freshwater below sea level. Geological evidence shows that the waters of the Mediterranean Sea gushed saltwater through a small channel into the Black Sea, eliminating its original shoreline. Today, the seashells on the beaches of the Black Sea are of marine life from saltwater. But modern technology has allowed humans to send mini submarines deeper, and they've found shells of freshwater mollusks, proving once more that a flood could've mixed these two types of water environments.

In 2000, the marine scientist responsible for uncovering the Titanic wreck led an underwater exploration of the Black Sea looking for proof of an ancient flood. Deep in the dark waters, they were amazed to find a wooden house collapsed by mud, along with tools and ceramics that gave evidence there was once human habitation around the time of the Great Flood that was taken by the force of water.

In 2007, in China, thousands of miles to the east, a geologist found evidence of human remains caused by a flood near the Yellow River around 2000 B.C. That seems like a huge gap in the distance between what was found at the Black Sea and what was found in China. The Bible's timeline calculates the flood to have occurred approximately 1656 A.M. (Anno Mundi, i.e., year of the world), or 2348 B.C. Since Genesis only gives us the ages of the patriarchs in terms of years, not months, this number could also vary by an additional six months for each generation. In addition, the dating of the human remains could be off by a few hundred years.

There's a 350-year difference between the Genesis flood and the evidence from China that also suggests that earthquakes and a tremendous amount of water caused a great catastrophe. We could debate the science of dating, but the difference isn't worth the argument. However, the 1,500-year difference between the Genesis flood and the remnants in the Black Sea may cause some to scrap the idea that these events are connected. However, the items found at the bottom of the Black Sea have been submerged in muck that is as old as the earth.

There have been discrepancies over the years in the accuracy of dating objects. Whether the carbon elements of the timeline are unknown or the artifacts found were not uniformly exposed to carbon in the atmosphere, there seem to be disagreements about carbon dating artifacts. The dating process can be off by hundreds or even thousands of years, so events that happened a very long time ago might be closer in years than is generally believed.

Moreover, the carbon dating calibration becomes untestable in the absence of written historical data to correlate all the factors that must be aligned to make the dating correct. In Chapter 8 I will discuss carbon dating and how the system of testing is skewed, and relate it to creation's timeline.

In this chapter we have learned about the commonality of the Flood across the world, including maps showing potential alternate routes, the possibility of multiple arks, a spot where someone may have left their altar behind, and even the mound where Noah built the ark. The evidence suggests that the Flood was of such importance that God gave plenty of warning. The people who sailed in the Ark(s) did not originate in Mesopotamia or anywhere close. The information here about the Flood only adds more to the previous chapter's theory that the Garden of Eden started elsewhere, like North America.

Plus, if we believe that Noah probably landed in a lower location, that will change where we believe some of our ancestors headed after the door of the Ark opened. Did everyone stay together? No, because we are so spread out today. But one story of man tells about a group that wanted to stay put until God made them leave. The scriptures make it clear that man is to use all of this world and not get stuck in one place.

CHAPTER VI

A Tower to God

"If it had been possible to build the Tower of Babel without
climbing it, it would have been permitted."
—*Franz Kafka*

THE NEXT BIG story in Genesis could explain how our species ended up spread across the globe and how we developed multiple language variations. But it, too, leaves us without much to go on for finding proof. The Tower of Babel has left many searching for its epic skyscraper. However, before leading you down another rabbit hole toward the proposed new location of the Tower of Babel, let us refresh this fascinating story.

On any typical Protestant Sunday, one could be taught the iconic story in the eleventh chapter of Genesis, the short tale of God's power and how mankind had gathered in one land to build a great tower to reach the Heavens in the clouds. It's another story of God's disapproval and the consequences for man. Typically, we are told that God stopped the Tower from being finished by confusing the people's language, which left them incapable of understanding each other. And then they scattered across the lands in different directions. Simple, right? Of course not.

This story seems cut and dried, except when you read each verse and know what we've learned from the previous chapters—that there is always more to the story. Let us look at the scriptures,

GENESIS 11:1 – 9:

¹ And the whole earth was of one language, and of one speech.

² And it came to pass, as they journeyed from the east, that they found a plain in the land of Shinar; and they dwelt there.

³ And they said one to another, Go to, let us make brick, and burn them thoroughly. And they had brick for stone, and slime had they for mortar.

⁴ And they said, Go to, let us build us a city and a tower, whose top may reach unto heaven; and let us make us a name, lest we be scattered abroad upon the face of the whole earth.

⁵ And the Lord came down to see the city and the tower, which the children of men builded.

⁶ And the Lord said, Behold, the people is one, and they have all one language; and this they begin to do: and now nothing will be restrained from them, which they have imagined to do.

⁷ Go to, let us go down, and there confound their language, that they may not understand one another's speech.

⁸ So the Lord scattered them abroad from thence upon

the face of all the earth: and they left off to build the city.

⁹ Therefore is the name of it called Babel; because the Lord did there confound the language of all the earth: and from thence did the Lord scatter them abroad upon the face of all the earth.

After going over the scriptures in Genesis, we find that the Tower's purpose was far greater than building a basic brick and mortar structure to reach the Heavens to walk the streets of gold. To break it down, let us go verse by verse:

GENESIS 11:1 – First, it's plausible that there were people in different parts of the world, especially since a great amount of time had passed since the Flood. The wording "all over the world" tells us that not all of those generations of people dwelt in the city later called Babel.

GENESIS 11:2 – As just mentioned, some time had passed since the passengers left the Ark, and people had begun to journey to new lands. Typically, we are taught that they left Mount Ararat and went east, but this verse states they journeyed from the east, which evidently means that they went in an opposite direction from east. The following maps show Mount Ararat in relation to the plain of Shinar (Mesopotamia), which is clearly south of it.

Current believed location of Shinar to Mount Ararat

A small crowd disagrees with the standard belief that Shinar is located in the Mesopotamia area and has Sumerian origins with Babylonian ties. It is known that the Sumerian people referred to their own country as "KI-EN-GIR," not even close to Shinar. Furthermore, the Babylonians called their ancestors "Sumeru." Also not close to Shinar. In-

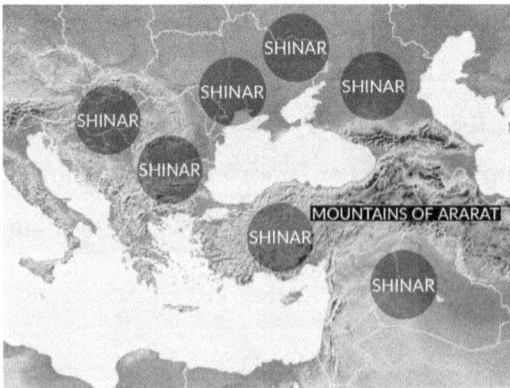

Possibilities of other Shinar locations

depth etymology of the name leads some to believe that Shinar is closer to China, while others think we haven't found it yet. Based on what verse 2 says, along with where Noah could've possibly landed (from the previous chapter), our options could literally change directions. The next map will show several plains where Shinar could be located.

> GENESIS 11:3 – The people who settled in the area of Babel decided they wanted to build a city of brick and mortar, along with a tower whose top could reach Heaven. First, using manmade bricks and mortar instead of natural stones suggests that these people wanted to show their God that they could make it on their own. It also shows they were advanced enough to manipulate earth into bricks. Second, these people could have climbed the nearest mountain faster than building a tower high enough to reach the clouds, or they could have gone back up into the mountains of Ararat to reach God. With everything these people had been told about their ancestors on the Ark, we can assume they were well aware that God didn't live on a cloud and that they couldn't easily build that high up. Therefore, "reaching" Heaven could be more about creating a direct line of communication, sort of how our cell phone towers work.

I know you're thinking the idea that they could send a signal to God is too advanced, but with the theoretical science concept of torsion fields, it's very possible. Simply put, torsion fields are direct energy sources that can travel through planets without losing strength. We will explain a little more in depth about this theoretical science later, along with other examples of where this energy could be found.

For now let us continue to break down the verses about Babel.

> GENESIS 11:4 – The people of this vast city wanted to reach
> Heaven to give themselves a reputation as a people and
> possibly break away from God so they wouldn't have to
> follow the commandment in Gen. 1:27-28 to spread their
> people across the Earth. As I said, they wanted a direct line
> of communication to God to state their case. Their ruler at
> the time, Nimrod, the great-grandson of Noah, not only
> ruled this city but also was presented in the Bible as a king
> of many nations. Babel was only the beginning, yet there is
> no historical evidence of who he truly was.

> GENESIS 11:5-7 – In these verses, God came to Earth to see the
> building of the Tower and the people. They give us insight
> into how God operates and how physical a being He truly
> is, especially if He had to come down for a closer look at
> the children of men. What was so interesting that he came
> to Earth? It tells us in the scriptures that the people of this
> city were of one language and purpose, and that nothing
> would keep them from accomplishing anything they could
> imagine. Therefore, God had to change their language to
> stop their progression. But why? The nations in today's
> world understand each other, and our advancements are
> quite great, so could the culture of this city have been more
> advanced in different ways than we are now?

GENESIS 11:8-9 – The people were scattered across the face of the Earth away from the city they built, known as Babel. The key word "thence" in this verse, defined as "from this place" or "from this time," reiterates that the people of Babel were confounded and made to leave that area for quite a time. Also, they were leaving an unfinished tower.

If they left the area for a while, it would further prove that Babylon, the area where most believe Babel was set, was most likely not the tall tower's location. Especially since Babylon was known for its high population as early as 1800 B.C. It's more likely that Babylon was the landing spot for some of the refugees after their languages changed, including Nimrod. Which would correlate with a stone tablet found 100 years ago in the ancient city of Babylon, in Iraq, about 80 miles south of Baghdad.

Tablet found in Iraq

Recent translations of the tablet depict the image of a large ziggurat, or step pyramid, and a civilization with great desires. Proof of Babel? Probably not. The representation of King Nebuchadnezzar throws the timeline off. The Bible tells us that Babel happened sometime after the Flood and before Abraham. We know that Abraham was ten generations after Noah, and Nebuchadnezzar was the king of Babylon around 604 B.C. This tablet more likely depicts members of the Babel group who tried to duplicate the tower years later after being separated from their families, friends, and fellow craftsmen.

Given the scarceness of clues, solving the mystery of where this lost landmark of the Bible has been hiding won't be easy. After the doors of the Ark open, Noah and his family are told to replenish the earth, not just Shinar. In addition, little clues tell us that after a time, Noah's sons went in different directions.

Genesis 10 gives us the generations of Noah's three sons (Shem, Ham, and Japheth). The first son mentioned, Japheth, speaks of 14 descendants; verse 5 says, *"By these were the isles of the Gentiles divided in their lands; every one after his tongue, after their families, in their nations."* It's believed that this group was divided into two main settlements of people, one headed in the direction of India and the other toward Europe. Verse 5 also suggests that one of these groups was a part of Babel: *"...divided in their lands; every one after his tongue ..."*

There is also a connection to Babel through the descendants of Noah's son Ham in Genesis 10:8-10, which mentions Nimrod, the grandson of Ham;

GENESIS 10:8 – 10

⁸ And Cush begat Nimrod: he began to be a mighty one in the earth.

⁹ He was a mighty hunter before the LORD: wherefore it is said, Even as Nimrod the mighty hunter before the LORD.

¹⁰ And the beginning of his kingdom was Babel, and Erech, and Accad, and Calneh, in the land of Shinar.

Since Nimrod was born soon after the Flood, it's reasonable to believe that he left the area to set up a kingdom in Babel and returned to rule the area of Shinar after the separation from the tower. It's also reasonable to assert that an overlap of the descendants of Japheth were a part of Babel under Nimrod's rule. If Babel was his first kingdom, then he didn't stay there to rule. He went on with his people to rule *Erech, and Accad, and Calneh in the land of Shinar.* The people of Ham are believed to have settled not only in Mesopotamia but also in northwestern Africa, the Arabian Peninsula, and Egypt.

Babel could literally be anywhere outside of Asia and the Americas.

When the people of Babel left, their communication was hindered, so it's safe to assume they didn't take time to disassemble the tower before leaving. Therefore, wherever the Tower of Babel was standing, the remains could still be there.

Though technology can scour our planet from above and penetrate to a great depth below us, we have not physically explored every inch of the Earth. There is more to this planet than the desert for all things in the Bible to have taken place. Clues to finding the true location of Babel would require some specific things. First, it would need to appear like the remnants of a step pyramid, or a similar manmade structure. With a few thousand years of vegetation, tall trees may conceal the tower from casual sight, but there would be a silhouette of a structure much like a pyramid. Furthermore, we would find other structures resembling an ancient city, including signs of a civilization, since the Tower of Babel came toward the end of this great city's development.

Also, this particular city was noted for its unstoppable potential and its people's unwillingness to spread across the world. So it's plausible that it was near natural resources, such as freshwater, fertile land for growing crops and feeding livestock, and well-forested areas to supply building materials. With these major factors considered, I'd like to examine one location, a highly controversial spot where such a tower could've been started. It's in Southern Europe, along the path of Japheth's descendants and close to where Ham's generations are believed to have gone.

A site in Bosnia holds several uniquely shaped mountains that fit the checklist of what we need. However, archeologists stand on different sides of the fence concerning this location. While some see only mountains, others believe this place is much more. They have gone so far as to claim that it's home to a pyramid and a few smaller buildings. The argument with the most voices claims that these are naturally occurring flatiron mountains, not pyramids or any type of manmade structures, even though they line up with the cardinal sides (north-south, east-west), which is a characteristic of other pyramids. Regardless, several curious minds wanted to make sure there wasn't more beneath the surface.

For more than twelve years, many archaeologists, energy researchers, and other interested parties have been studying this area in Bosnia, which is located northwest of the mountain range of Ararat. This region was once covered with forest plateaus, along with rich soil and rocks, making the terrain less likely to erode, keeping it fertile for agriculture, and making it suitable for setting a foundation. There is easy access to a multitude of glacier lakes and major rivers, and the lands are rife with natural springs that are tapped today for bottling water. This sounds like a great place to set up a permanent community. This controversial gem, located in Visoko, Bosnia, has become known as the Bosnian Pyramid.

Over the years of studying this area, many images have been taken from the air and space, revealing other potential structures with similar triangular sides. In addition, thermal inertia testing—measuring how quickly or slowly an object gains or loses heat in its environment—suggests that these structures are denser than the surrounding mountains and appear thermally cooler inside. Adding to the argument that these are manmade buildings and not mere flatiron mountains is the fact that they consist of hallways and chambers that contribute to the measured heat loss.

Only scant geological analysis was allowed in 2005-2007, but results confirmed layers of manually cut sandstone and breccia blocks within the structures. This breccia block is composed of gravel, sandstone, and shale with an element much like cement to bind the bricks. From the parts geologists were able to observe, a manmade mortar was applied after the stones were processed and layered perfectly together. Sounds a lot like what was described in Genesis 11:3.

Aside from the appearance and signs of manmade brick and mortar, the area around the suggested pyramid and its smaller structures is littered with sidewalks and what seems to be an interlocking tunnel system beneath all the buildings. Whatever this area was during its ancient existence, it was massive and meant to tower above its neighboring mountain ranges. And it had air-conditioned tunnels.

Underground tunnels at Visoko

Evidence that humans were capable of building massive structures predates the Flood. Even the massive undertaking of building an Ark(s) would have been a project that God knew man could achieve. Therefore, it makes sense that those saved from the waters also possessed the knowledge to build the same types of structures. This led me to think that the Tower of Babel had to be an enormous megastructure, larger than the Ark, larger than the pyramids we stand in awe of today, and somewhere away from the known areas in the Middle East.

Using modern technology to map this area reveals that the Bosnian Pyramid would surpass the Pyramid of Giza by more than 250 feet. Furthermore, this structure is in a location that was abandoned thousands of years ago and not settled by humans again until around the 4th century B.C.

Visoko, Bosnia, has been the graveyard of a large step pyramid and perhaps a few smaller ones hidden from the world until 2005, when a man looked at the peculiar shape of the mountain and thought it was something more. Because we lack complete information, many reject the notion that this site might have been the home of the Tower of Babel. Nevertheless, there is ample evidence that a great structure was begun here.

The scriptures are clear that the languages of the people were changed, but it says nothing about their minds or their ability to function being altered. Therefore, why wouldn't it be understood that these people scattered and tried to rebuild based on what they already knew from building the city and the Tower of Babel? Even though these people were still extremely intelligent after their languages were confounded, they lacked all the pieces to collectively do things exactly the same way they did them at Babel. This provides insight into how megastructures, like the pyramids of Egypt, are similar to other step pyramids across the globe. It's plausible that the design of all pyramids originated at Babel and spread from there. If the first pyramid was located in Babel, its people would have separately taken with them only pieces of knowledge about how to build the structure. Thus, they would have been unable to duplicate it, because the brick makers could no longer understand the architects.

If a part of the construction team at Babel understood each other's new language enough to head south together toward the desert, they could've been involved in designing Egypt's wonders and in any attempts in Iraq to rebuild under the rule of Nebuchadnezzar, as depicted on the tablet. This would be another connection to their desire to build almost perfect geometric structures so long ago.

Anyone who left the Ark and traveled in a different direction also would have understood how to create such magnificent step pyramid towers but would have had a purpose other than defying God. Speaking of the other post-Flood cultures, there is evidence in many countries that civilizations began around the same time. For example, there is evidence of pyramid-like structures in Brazil.

The structures found in Brazil date to 3000 B.C. and are older than the Egyptian ones by a few hundred years. For years archeologists looked at these merely as piles of seashell rubbish, allowing many to be plowed over for roadways. However, a closer look revealed that these were meticulously constructed with a pyramid design.

"Our new research shows that Brazil's prehistoric Indians 5,000 years ago were more sophisticated than we had thought and were capable of producing truly monumental structures," said Professor Edna Morley, director of the Instituto do Patrimonio Historico e Artistico Nacional (National Heritage Institute), in Santa Catarina, where most of the Brazilian pyramids have been discovered. "These massive structures will help revolutionize the way we think about ancient Indian cultures," she added.

Many places that our history books overlook reveal evidence that the abilities of ancient humans were greater than we once assumed. If we believe in Adam and Eve, then we understand that they were shut out of Eden for partaking of the fruit that would make them wise. This wisdom wasn't taken from them when they left Eden's gate. Throughout the years we have found younger structures that were hidden from the world, just like the structures in Visoko that prove such knowledge.

The next images show what archeologists were led to by locals when told about ancient civilizations. You can see that in just a couple thousand years, these places were almost swallowed by forests, making it very likely that the Tower of Babel would be unrecognizable as a structure.

The following images are of the actual cornerstone and pathways uncovered in Bosnia. The project to uncover the building faces many hurdles, including skeptics, and the results have been slowed down.

Stone path of the pyramid in Bosnia

Artifact found in Visoko, Bosnia

If the manmade pieces aren't enough to convince nonbelievers, the measurable facts should give them pause. Earlier I mentioned torsion field energy. In the late 1800s, Nikola Tesla hypothesized a way to communicate through the stars, known as torsion field of standing energy. This hypothesis states that a standing energy from the Earth could be used like electricity and directed into the cosmos faster and stronger than light, like a cellphone to the Gods. The theory is that torsion fields exist everywhere, even in the human body, but finding them and harnessing this power is still considered pseudoscience.

Interestingly, one of the researchers and experts on the Bosnian Pyramid project, Dr. Semir Osmanagić, found those types of waves on top of the Bosnian pyramid. He claims that these waves are 10 billion times faster than the speed of light and able to pass through the stars and planets.

"The discovery of Tesla's standing waves at the top of the Bosnian Pyramid of the Sun—which are believed to travel faster than the speed of light, while not losing strength as they pass through cosmic bodies—prove the existence of something referred to as a cosmic web or cosmic internet, which allow for an immediate intergalactic communication throughout the universe," writes Dr. Osmanagić.

What does this mean for the Tower of Babel being located in Bosnia? As previously mentioned, I believe the people of Babel were trying to build a communication device to talk with God, and this discovery lends evidence to support this theory and stacks the side in favor of Bosnia being the location of Babel. The next chapter will explain more about torsion theory, along with other hypotheses that link science and religion in an effort to uncover the truth about the treasures the world lost track of.

I will always step outside the circle to find answers, especially when the only information we are told to follow has been translated repeatedly by men who weren't there to see the actual events. The next chapter will dive into how science parallels history and God. The stories we have been told of our ancient world may change as we line everything up together.

CHAPTER VII

Science, Religion, and Unseen Energy

"The more I study science, the more I believe in God."
—*Albert Einstein*

OVER THE YEARS, high-powered telescopes have focused on our universe. We wonder how far we can see past our own orbit and contemplate the potential for other life, even as we put Earth's Creators under a microscope to disprove their existence. Now, as we attempt to unravel the mysteries this planet has been holding, things are starting to merge, as science and divine creation are seen as one, making God the ultimate scientist.

When trying to link how the events of Genesis correlate with what we've learned to date, one needs to remember that the way the world looks now is not how it looked with Pangea. Our planet has undergone repeated changes over billions of years. This is a VERY important point to remember as we proceed! This planet is probably more than billions of years old, but so many cling to 6,000 or 7,000 years, as many have been taught to believe.

The chronology of Genesis deals with fixed dates of the various events recorded after creation. For the earliest parts of Old Testament history we rely entirely on the scriptures; but the Hebrew Bible, the Septuagint or Greek translation, and the Samaritan Pentateuch do not agree with one another, so dates can't be fixed with certainty.

However, regardless of what you believe, there's no denying that if a God is infinite, his creations are older than we can fathom.

It's not hard to see why many believers in God(s) are looking to the modern teachings of man concerning the theory of human origin. What separates science and religion? Science typically brings us tangible, or at least measurable, results, and many people accept every word written by scientists. However, science does not always produce consistent beliefs. That's why most elements of science linger in the realm of hypothesis rather than becoming scientific laws. Same with religion, no one can agree on who God is and how we all got here, and when science claimed that we evolved from a lesser species, it put distance between science and church doctrines, resulting in conflict between religion and science.

Equally, there is a movement away from theories of man. It's easy to lose trust in science when theories change repeatedly over the years. For example, before the world clung to the Big Bang theory, there was Einstein's Static Universe. The idea was that the universe had a fixed volume and was a closed system. Einstein not only was in favor of this theory, but he also developed it into the theory of general relativity.

Though a small group of scientists still adheres to this model, the modern notion came after the Hubble telescope saw the heavenly bodies moving away from us. Yet even this ever-expanding universe is still a hypothesis because no one is certain. As far as we know, there could be multiple universes like ours, enclosed within a specific space that is always in motion, with other galaxies orbiting at variable rates around one central point where God lives; but that sounds ridiculous, so we won't go there today.

A great deal of knowledge preceded us that we have yet to grasp.

Ancient civilizations were able to harness unique energy and find their way around the planet. Granted, they weren't distracted by their smartphones or what's streaming on television, so they had more time to focus on the world around them.

If we stayed where science first took us, we would be standing by waiting for spontaneous generation of life or making cold fusion systems on our countertops. Science isn't any more reliable than religion, and as I've said before, both rely on faith. But we still use it to understand what we don't know for sure and take it on faith until it changes. No matter what side you stand on, science has advanced farther in technology than what we could've imagined a century ago, which proves that we can't predict what will or won't be discovered in the future.

At least with religion, people tend to stay constant within their own beliefs. People stand behind their God(s), even if they don't know everything about him. Science, on the other hand, has had its share of wardrobe changes.

Let's take the dinosaurs, for example; what has science taught us about these extinct creatures other than that they lived an unimaginably long time ago?

Growing up, some of us were taught that dinosaurs walked the Earth millions of years ago in different stages before man and became extinct before we arrived. Theories of the demise of these giant creatures have changed over the years.

In 1928 it was believed that dust clouds blocked UV rays, reducing vitamin D in vegetation, which prevented the dinosaurs from getting the nutrients needed to survive. Since then, hypotheses have ranged from poison to fungus to cold weather to insects eating all the plant life to volcanoes to glaciers to meteorites to our latest hypothesis, a huge asteroid that hit Earth near the Yucatan Peninsula in Central America and wiped out the dinosaurs. The following map shows where the asteroid hit and where dinosaur fossils have so far been uncovered.

Area of claimed asteroid that wiped out the dinosaurs

You can see that this idea doesn't quite fit. Though the impact of this asteroid would've killed dinosaurs, or anything else, for that matter, it would only be within a certain vicinity of the impact site. Therefore, this hypothesis has now evolved to include deadly gases that were produced after the asteroid hit, which changed the climate and the vegetation to exterminate these creatures. Still, I find it impressive that the gases were strong enough to spread across the globe; even if dinosaurs existed during Pangea, it would've been difficult for the gases to spread. Also, the gas only destroyed particular dinosaurs, leaving a few of the smaller ones behind to go on to exist today. Unless you believe there was a restart on dinosaurs much like the Flood, or that all the bones are fake—but let's not go there.

The point isn't to debate the death of the dinosaurs; it's to show that while scientists are some of the planet's smartest people, they do not know everything. Most things are purely good guesses until someone comes up with something better. My guess is that the magnetic poles reversed and the planet's climate shifted in certain areas. North and south literally flipped.

Is that possible? Yes, and it has happened many times on this planet throughout its years in existence.

Here is where a lot of people get lost. The merry-go-round of ideas that we think up sound crazier when we throw the words "millions or billions of years ago" after explaining something. People can't fathom that many years ago, so it's hard to see things being in the same time structure written in a couple of verses in Genesis.

According to current science, tectonic shifts caused the major changes in the landscape of our planet over hundreds of thousands of years. The topography and the places we've become comfortable knowing may not have been so when Adam and Eve were placed in the Garden of Eden, and it probably looked a lot different even before that. The notion that the face of the Earth wasn't reshaped overnight may not be accurate. I agree that much of what changed topographically and environmentally took a long time, but the alterations from Eden to when Noah parked the Ark might have been drastic over the year they were on the boat.

We have discussed Pangea and the idea of continental drift, but to further prove this happened, let's look at Antarctica. Today our southernmost continent is covered in solid ice, and we don't expect to find much life outside of penguins and a few scientists.

Nevertheless, in 1912 a team was led to the cold white lands of the South Pole, where they found proof that at one time Antarctica had a warmer continent. Fossils of dinosaurs and seed ferns prove that this land was full of life, and this evidence also connects it to other lands (Australia, India, and Africa) because they bear the same seed fern along their borders.

Remember where Antarctica was on the map of Pangea? Notice which continents are connected to its borders: Australia, India, and Africa.

Pangea rendering with Antarctica at the bottom

This shows not only that these lands were once close and that Pangea was closely shaped like this, but also that on the grand scale of Creation, these places were together after God created life in verse 11:

Genesis 1:11

¹¹ And God said, "Let the earth bring forth grass, the herb yielding seed, and the fruit tree yielding fruit after his kind, whose seed is in itself, upon the earth: and it was so."

Plate tectonics and continental drift theories are abundantly confusing; unknowns include how fast or slow a land mass can move, and how fast or slow it could build up mountains. Theories can fluctuate depending on whether you believe continents have their own plates or whether you believe plates are interchangeable between continents. Since these are purely hypotheses, we can't say this is actually how the Earth was reshaped; these are just good guesses.

The challenge arises when good guesses are used as a standard in trying to figure out other mysteries. New theories about our Earth are constantly being published and gathering followers, whether they are right or wrong. Even now, after we've reached space and watched the Earth spin, there are people like the Flat Earthers, who have quite the following as well as a set of scientific processes to prove their idea that the earth is flat. Proof of truth doesn't change everyone's mind.

One scientific finding that could change how we see direction in the scriptures is a discovery closer to our recognizable timeline. It is the way we can find our bearings on Earth today. Most think that the magnetic north of a compass and true north are the same place on Earth, but they're not. In fact, they're several thousand kilometers apart. The following map shows magnetic north as of 2015 in comparison with true north.

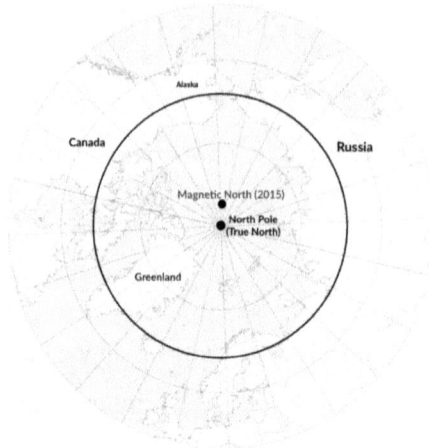

Magnetic north and true north

Not only are they separated by miles, but magnetic north, the area to which your compass points, is always moving. Modern GPS settings are set up with calculations of declination angles that are always updating. If you're not using technology, be sure to use a current map when you're in unfamiliar territory, especially when going long distances.

Typically, it's measured at around 10 kilometers a year, but it seems to have picked up to 40 kilometers a year. Its current path is headed toward Russia, as you can see in the next image. True north, or the North Pole, is the direct point on earth that is geographically positioned on the northern top of Earth. It's the position that our planet rotates from, and it doesn't change. The next map shows where magnetic north has been over the last 200 years.

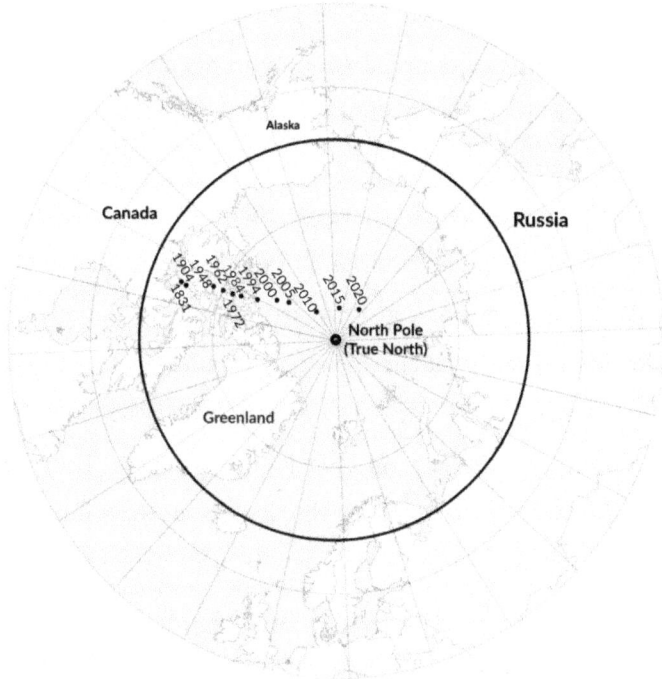

Scientists are not certain why this happens. There are many good hypotheses but no actual facts to show why magnetic north and the Earth's axis poles are not one and the same. Current notions say fluctuations in the Earth's magnetic core cause it to move, but since we don't know for certain what's at the center of the Earth's core, any hypothesis sounds likely.

What does this have to do with what we've been talking about? A few things come to mind when we consider change in navigation being an issue. For example, where is east of Eden or eastward from Ararat? We can claim that this was based on their own source of navigation, but when we also claim that the scriptures were guided by God, we have to accept that he knew which way magnetic north was.

Almost anyone can learn to read a map and calculate the

directions of declination between magnetic north and true north with their position, but it takes preparation, training, and knowing what the lands look like topographically. For accuracy, one would need to discover that a magnetic north exists and that it's moving. For a while, some European explorers thought their compass needles were following the North Star or an island in the Arctic. It wasn't until 1831 that explorers started pinning down its location in the Arctic Circle. Later it was realized that it had moved its location in 1903.

Scholars believe the ancient people followed the sun, the moon, and the stars to guide them on long journeys, much as the wise men followed the bright star toward the birthplace of Christ. Genesis doesn't always give clues to every season in which the stories are being told, leaving plenty of leeway regarding the actual origins of Eden, the landing of the Ark, and location of Babel if we rely solely on the words *north*, *east*, *south*, and *west*.

As far as knowing where magnetic north was during the time of Genesis, we can only speculate, since its movements are unknown. Some feel that this random movement is a natural movement that will come back around, while others believe that this could cause a pole reversal very soon.

These thoughts about magnetic north and its scientific unpredictability made me instantly think of magnetic fields and their role in a pseudoscience known as torsion energy fields. This type of energy will help explain how the Tower of Babel would've been able to communicate through the universe, if the builders had completed the pyramid.

Let's break this down and try to make it easier to understand. The following is a simple way to view Earth's magnetic field and its invisible waves from the outside. As you can see in the diagram, the Earth rotates westerly.

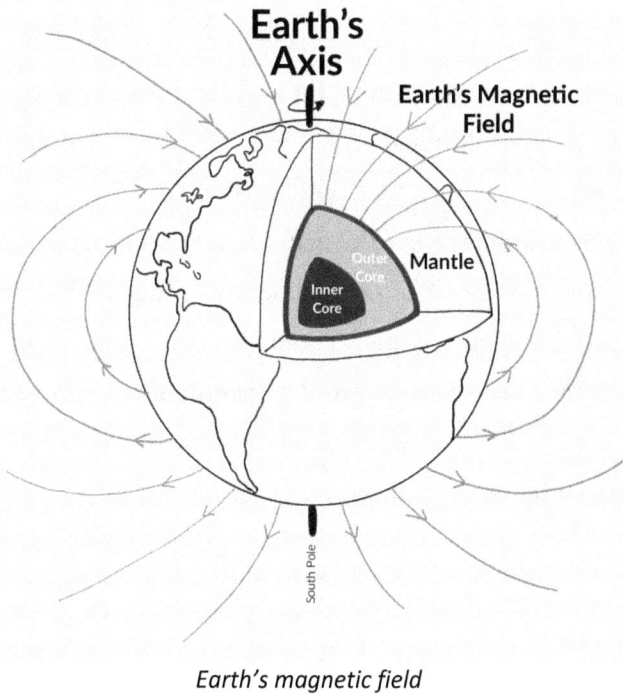

Earth's magnetic field

It is believed that the magnetic field penetrates Earth's surface deep into the mantle and possibly the outer liquid core. Then it continues its circulation back out through the opposite hemisphere.

The outer magnetic field waves protect us from harmful solar winds, but what about the waves that penetrate deeper inside Earth where the core is rotating faster and in an opposite direction? That's where nonphysical science comes in. I have a hypothesis that Earth is a large generator of torsion energy, that this energy field can be tapped, and that it was being tapped by ancient cultures, including the people of Babel.

We touched lightly on the subject of torsion field energy in the previous chapter, noting that Dr. Osmanagić claimed to have found torsion fields on top of the Bosnian pyramid. Basically, scientists like Nikolai Tesla theorized that the torsion, or the spinning rotation/twisting, of or inside of large objects could create a unique energy field that could penetrate through the cosmos without breaking down as it passes through solid objects. Much like the opposite twisting reaction between Earth and its core.

Imagine cutting Earth in half to see all the layers. As in the previous image, the next image outlines the magnetic field penetrating the mantle but shows it pulled into the outer core along with the generated torsion energy. Notice the opposite rotation between Earth and the core, as I mentioned, which is creating that twisting effect that emanates a different type of energy, or torsion energy.

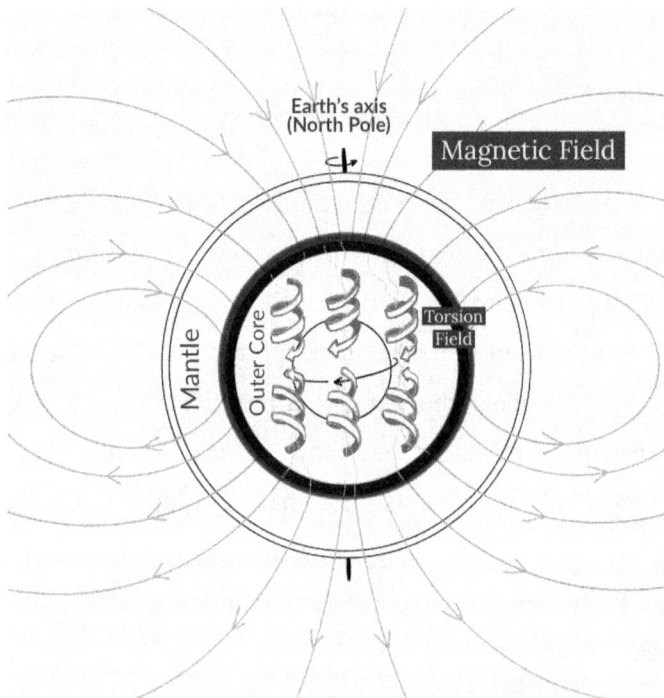

Inside Earth with magnetic and torsion fields

The next image illustrates how this energy is hypothetically tapped. Notice the channels of super positively charged water running throughout the structures in Bosnia, sandwiched between the negatively charged layers of the Earth. From the top there is a concentrated beam that looks like a strand of DNA, having a unique geometric spiral of combined energies that emanates from this world into the cosmos. I find fascinating the level of knowledge the ancients possessed to be able to control this energy.

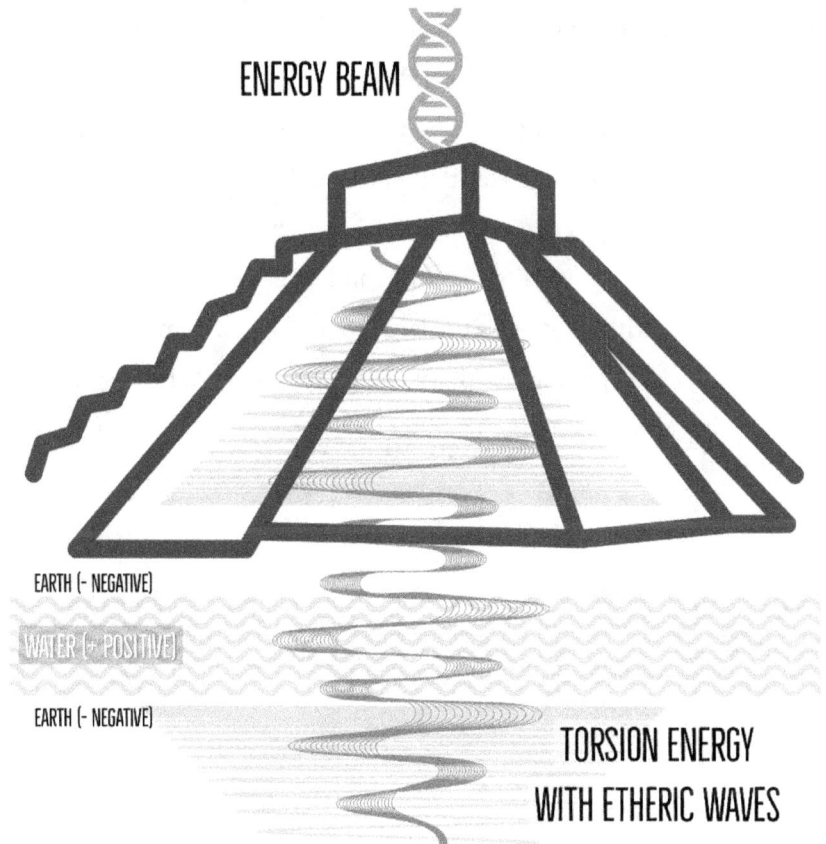

ENERGY BEAM

EARTH (- NEGATIVE)

WATER (+ POSITIVE)

EARTH (- NEGATIVE)

TORSION ENERGY
WITH ETHERIC WAVES

Researchers used scientific devices to record the beam coming out of the top of the unfinished pyramid in Bosnia, as shown in this image. It's believed to be a blend of torsion and etheric waves, or, more scientifically, a quantum vacuum. The current hypothesis is that these pyramids, and other pyramids, were created as healing stations of sorts across the world. I agree that was part of the purpose. But this particular pyramid is a massive energy station, so why worry about getting the beam stronger toward the top if you were merely healing inside where the energy wasn't as strong? This is why I feel this location would fit with the people of Babel needing to talk to God about continuing to live their lives there.

Since torsion energy is completely hypothetical, so are these statements. Regardless, I feel that the people of Babel knew how to generate this large energy beam, which they needed to heal their people within the other structures, and I believe they planned to communicate with God from the larger one. The next image shows the Bosnian Pyramid pulling out those energy waves into a helix-like effect toward the cosmos.

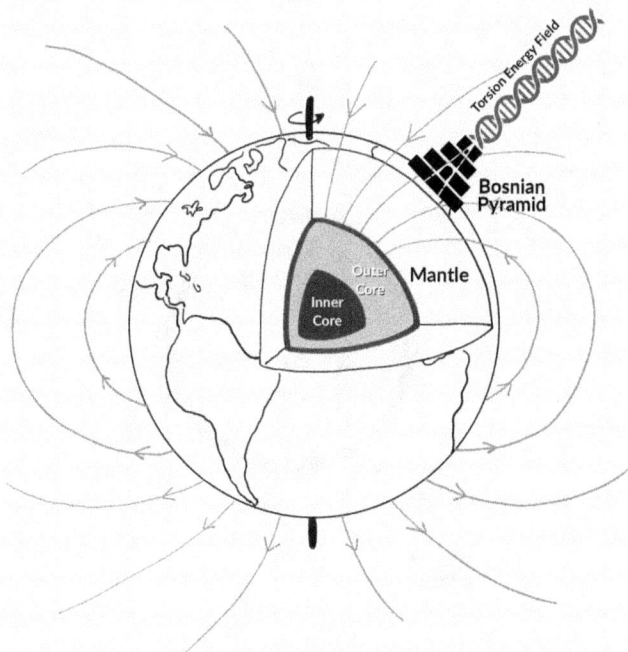

Bosnian pyramid pulling out energy fields

If energy is being pulled toward one location, then would Newton's third law, "For every action, there is an equal and opposite reaction," apply here? I continue my theory that there has to be an opposite reaction on the other side of the world.

Since I am not an expert on this subject, I reached out to a well-known electrical engineer, Goran Marjanovic, who is known for his research on Tesla's theoretical torsion field generators and on the Bosnian pyramid site. I asked him: If someone generates this much torsion energy in one spot, is there an opposite polar reaction on the other side of the world, as shown in the image?

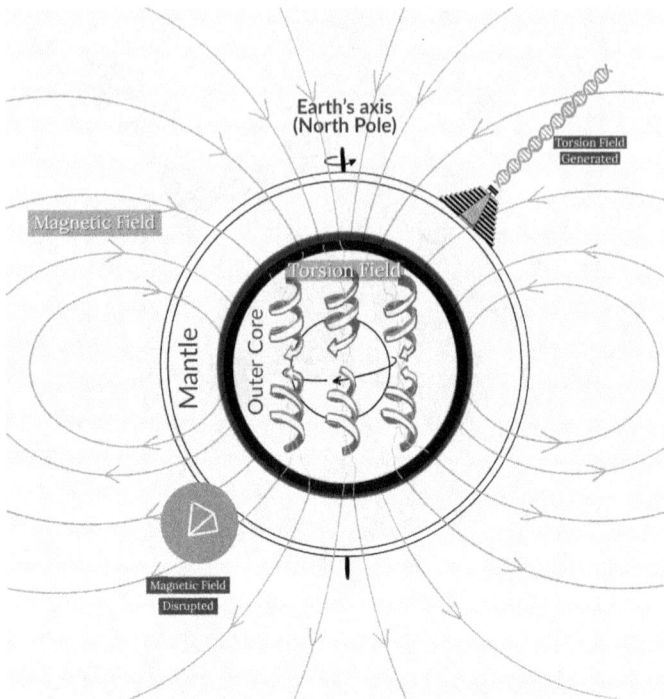

Polar opposite reaction to the Bosnian pyramid

He agreed: "Yes. This implies the involvement of the antipode in the process of forming a standing wave or a scalar field in the configuration where the planet Earth is used as a 'resonator'. What's more—besides the opposite point there is one more position of importance and that is the position defined by the cross-section of a parallel and a meridian—same one that passes through the Pyramid of the Sun on the opposite side of Earth." Goran Marjanovic, electrical engineer.

His added position of a parallel and meridian cross-section would look like the next image.

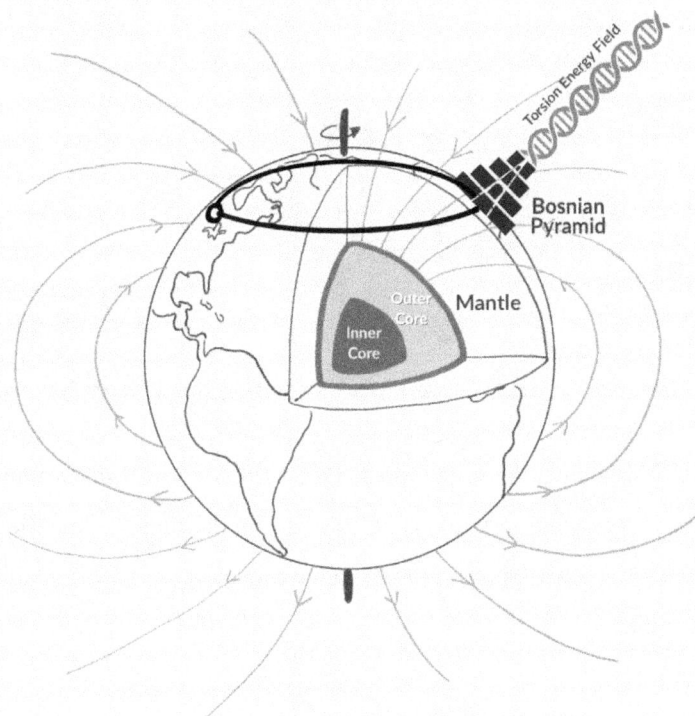

Cross-section position

Out of curiosity and a vague gut feeling, I plotted both points onto a map. If you haven't noticed, I have a thing for maps. The next image shows the Bosnian Pyramid cross-section parallel point in the Northern Hemisphere south of Alaska, and the antipode is located in the Southern Hemisphere approximately 850 miles from New Zealand.

Antipode and cross-section parallel points of the Bosnian Pyramid

What is amazing about these two opposite locations is how close they are to nearby vortices. Like the famous Bermuda Triangle, these two areas are part of a 12-piece collection of areas where planes and ships vanish.

Points in relation to nearby vortices

There are five in the northern and five in the southern, along with North and South Poles, that are evenly distributed across the lines of latitude.

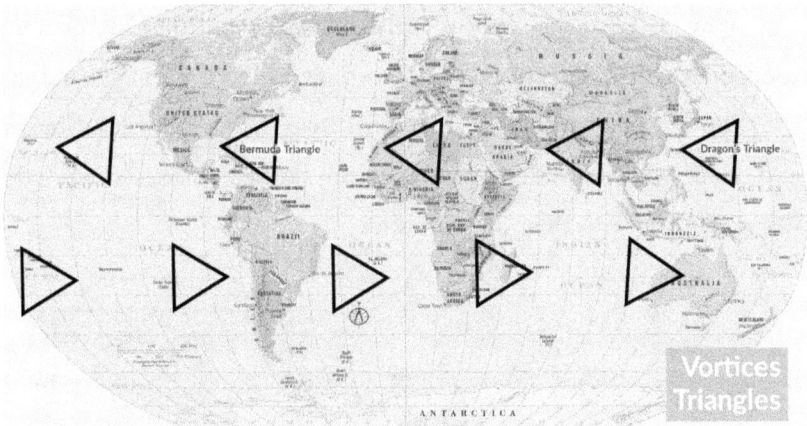

Vortices across the world (North and South Pole not represented)

These anomalies have puzzled scientists over the years, and many ideas have been thrown out as reasons for all the electromagnetic interference. I don't know how they came into existence, but note how perfectly they are placed. It's hard to see this on a 2D map of the world, but in the next image I have connected each triangle vortex to its own antipode (its opposite), which is another triangle vortex.

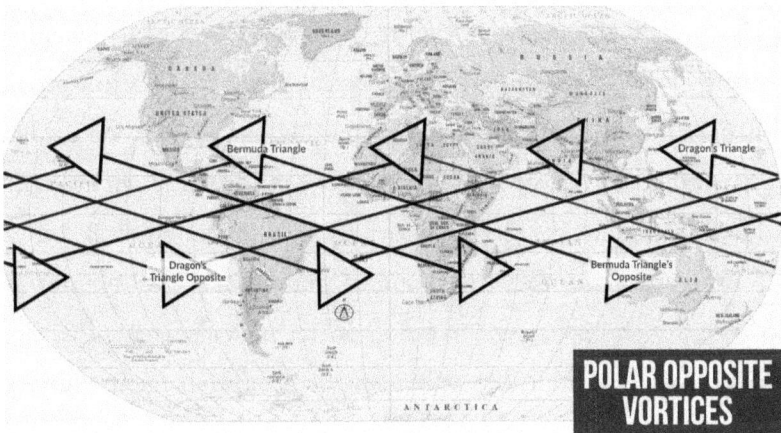

Polar opposites of vortices

Why do I feel the need to explain this? This further supports my thoughts that the ancient people knew how to tap this energy and use it to communicate with God. The next map shows how other known and unknown civilizations that built in random places around the world stack up with their opposite sites.

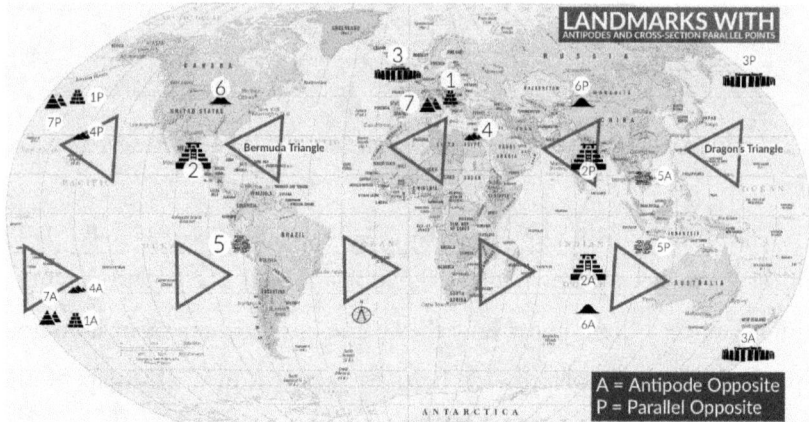

1-Bosnian Pyramid, 2-Mayan Structures, 3-Stonehenge, 4-Egyptian Pyramids, 5-Nazca Lines, 6-Monks Mound, 7-Mediterranean Pyramids

For those feeling like this was a screenplay from a science-fiction movie, know that humans do this all day long. The body is much like an energy generator. Our energy is so strong that it can affect people without us saying anything. The way our body is aligned, we are like living pyramids. This is why it is good to be in control of our thoughts and feelings and to take care of the acidity levels of our physical body.

Every time we focus our minds, body, and souls to pray or meditate, we are repeating the action of the ancients, creating energy fields that we pull from the earth below us to supercharge it and send it.

Prayer and meditation can happen at any time and in any position, but there is a definite power when we kneel or bring our body into a more focused stance. In the Christian Bible there are many instances of praying, but in Luke 22:40-41 Jesus gives his example of his prayer to the Heavenly Father at the Mount of Olives before he is arrested. In his example he was kneeling.

LUKE 22:40 – 41

⁴⁰ And when he was at the place, he said unto them,
Pray that ye enter not into temptation.

[41] And he was withdrawn from them about a stone's cast, and kneeled down, and prayed,

All this speculation about torsion energy fields sound great when we are theorizing, but the scientific community as a whole has not accepted much evidence that torsion energy fields exist in this capacity. However, other speculative theories sparked research into the energy inside pyramids from a more terrestrial perspective, which proves it from the back side of the theory.

For example, former defense contractor and scientist Dr. Alexander Golod had been studying the effects of pyramids since 1990 in the Soviet Union. He constructed a 144-foot-high modern fiberglass pyramid near Moscow and others throughout Russia and Ukraine.

Modern Russian pyramid

This scientist used a wide spectrum of experiments in agriculture, physics, medicine, and health studies to understand the effects of pyramids. These studies have shown some promising results for our wellness, and they're accepted by the general science community. The following list is composed of a few of the results from the pyramid studies:

— *The immune system of organisms tested improved (blood leukocyte composition increased).*

— *Seeds that were stored in the pyramid for 1-5 days showed a 30%-100% increase in yield.*

— *There was improvement of the ozone above the area of one of the pyramids.*

— *Violent weather appears to decrease in the vicinity of the pyramids. Culture tests showed an increase in survival of cellular tissue after virus/bacteria infection.*

— *Radioactive substances show a decreased level of radiation inside the pyramid.*

— *Physicists observed significant changes in superconductivity temperature thresholds.*

— *Water remains liquid to minus 40 degrees Celsius but freezes instantly if bumped in any way.*

This list supports the premise that pyramids were built as healing stations. Another interesting discovery was that increasing the height of the pyramid improved the quality of the results. Imagine what the pyramid in Bosnia, at more than seven hundred feet high, would have produced; definitely something powerful enough to bring the Lord to Earth.

All this talk about unseen energy and pseudoscience ties into two other topics we spoke about earlier in the book: ghosts and UFOs. It's easy for us to accept terms like electricity and sound waves, because these are things we see and hear every day. Yet we cannot see sound waves, we just know they exist. The Bible is riddled with the power of sound waves and other unseen energy that can reshape the earth, bring down cities, or merely move the waves of the ocean.

For those of us who believe in a God, we cannot see him but we know that the energy of his presence is there. Whether you believe in angels or other unseen entities, we have to agree there is a lot we can't see that still exists. Ghosts, or spiritual entities, have an energy that some say can be caught with instruments that measure changes in energy fields. I feel that UFOs can also detect where these energy levels are around the world and use it to enter our atmosphere. None of this denies the existence of God; it simply magnifies his vast creation, emphasizes the system's perfection, and demonstrates how his promise of life after death is present still today.

It is easy to look away from the other side of things and stay safe on your own side of believing. Most scientists don't want to add a God factor to their equations any more than most people of faith want to consider science as a companion to understanding creation. I feel you have to accept both if you want that deeper knowledge.

There are things in this world that we can't easily comprehend. However, we have shown that people from all over the world are holding onto traditions of faith, but now they want more answers to clarify their purpose. We can't claim we have found Babel or the landing site of the Ark unless we truly understand where it all started. Until we agree where to find Eden.

CHAPTER VIII

Back to Eden

"Some beautiful paths can't be discovered without getting lost."
—*Erol Ozan*

IF YOU HAVEN'T recognized it, there is much about this world we haven't come to fully understand. We have much to learn about the natural forces that surround us, and what energy might be lingering below us or even above us. The builders of Babel, Egypt, Maya, and all the others who created mound/pyramid-like structures knew the power of this planet and were able to utilize it to become great civilizations for a time, but how did they know? The knowledge that came out of Eden is more potent than any library or search engine available today.

GENESIS 3:5

⁵ For God doth know that in the day ye eat thereof,
then your eyes shall be opened, and ye shall be as gods,
knowing good and evil.

Eden gave the first humans the knowledge level of God(s), and this knowledge was passed down through generations until it was lost somewhere along the way. In the initial chapter about Eden it was shown where the garden could've possibly been located based on unique landmarks, but why are these areas left with hauntings and visitors from other worlds? Could it be that there is a pathway to access torsion energy that spirits tap into? Are UFOs fueled by this energy? Another possibility is that visitors from distant galaxies are seeking the trees from the Garden of Eden that God left hidden. Regardless, we have a new direction on which to focus our research about these areas and what type of energy emanates from them.

Aside from possible archeological sites and energy to prove this area is significant to Eden, can we justify the existence of Eden within the natural understanding of the Genesis timeline? Let's journey back to see if her gates actually fit within Earth's timeline.

A big part of what separates religion and science is Earth's timeline. For those who get stuck on the millions of years it took to get our planet in the shape it's in right now, the timeline causes anxiety, especially if they think God only took six days to create the Earth. Anything before that doesn't quite fit into their rational thought. Well, get over it. Even though the notion that God is without age makes sense, humans have a hard time understanding "infinite" and how that works out for them.

Earth didn't just come into existence 6,000 to 7,000 years ago. It's more likely that our planet was created by God and covered by water for billions of years before God touched it with life. Let me explain. To begin, let's talk about the planet being covered by water. These verses written in Genesis make this statement plausible.

GENESIS 1:1 – 2

¹ In the beginning God created the heaven and the earth.

² And the earth was without form, and void; and
darkness was upon the face of the deep. And the Spirit of
God moved upon the face of the waters.

God knows everything, and everything wouldn't fit within the pages of the Bible. It would take trillions of books to explain creation. Therefore, the first verse is basic and a beautiful explanation that God created the universe. It doesn't say when and it doesn't say in what order. The planets he did create at this point were without the shapes we know today. If we read this as it's stated in verse 2, Earth was unformed, unfilled, dark, and wet. It also reaffirms what Peter said in 2 Peter 3, that the earth of then is not the earth of now.

2 PETER 3:5 – 6

⁵ For this they willingly are ignorant of, that by the
word of God the heavens were of old, and the earth
standing out of the water and in the water:

⁶ Whereby the world that then was, being overflowed
with water, perished:

Interestingly, technology is allowing science to catch a glimpse of this as astronomers witness the formation of stars and planets out of clouds of chaotic dust. The Spitzer Space telescope is a high-powered piece of equipment that uses infrared wavelengths to show scientists how the Gods create planets out of chaos, i.e., without form and void. The Spitzer telescope has given us evidence of two new planets born out there, confirming not only statements in Genesis but also that God has no end and that Earth probably isn't the only planet God will put life on.

Regarding the Earth being covered in water, as verse 2 insinuates, science has speculated over the years that our planet formed dry, and high impacts created a molten surface on the young Earth. Water came much later, with coincidental comets and asteroids carrying water. Now science has changed its tune, based on evidence from a nearby asteroid that carries a lot of water weight around her belt. Asteroids are believed to be broken planets, and it stands to reason that if they still carry water from the beginning, then so would any other planet with water. Thus, Earth may have also begun with water on her surface, as Genesis tells us.

The chapters of Genesis are littered with interesting, but boring, lines of genealogy and then random stories of humanity's creation and how humans struggled to learn to walk "upright" in the laws their God gave them. The struggle now is getting God's people to remember where they came from and how to get back to Eden.

As I previously said, the timeline of Earth gives people fits and makes it hard to agree that science and God's timeline are similar. Once God created our planet, I don't believe he instantly started placing life on her shores. Instead, our planet was created and then spent billions of years traveling through the expanse of the universe in a frozen or thawed state, making contact with other planets or other bodies, reshaping her until she was given a Sun to orbit and was ready to sustain life.

Once Earth was ready for life, we can argue the conceptual days of God's creation until we are blue in the face. God's time can be looked at through many perspectives, depending on whether Genesis is talking about Earth's rotation of one day equaling almost 24 hours or God's day that is said to last about 1,000 years. Most people assume that all planets spin, or rotate, at the same 23 hours, 56 minutes and 4 seconds that Earth rotates. In actuality, some take longer to make a complete day and others take less time to make a full day rotation.

For example, one day on Saturn would last less than eleven hours, but a day on Venus—one complete rotation—lasts approximately 243 Earth days. Why do they vary? Scientists can only speculate, but they believe it has a lot to do with the Sun's strong gravitational pull and Venus's thick atmosphere, but that isn't consistent throughout all the planets. The chart below lists the planets in order from the Sun and shows each planet's day—one complete rotation—in terms of Earth days and each planet's year—one complete revolution around the sun—in terms of Earth days or years. Yes, Pluto is included because no one can agree if he is a planet or not, so we will list him for fun.

PLANET	1 DAY ROTATION	1 YEAR REVOLUTION
Mercury	58.6 days	88 days
Venus	243 days	224 days
Earth	1 day	365 days
Mars	1.03 days	687 days
Jupiter	0.41 days	12 years
Saturn	0.45 days	29 years
Uranus	0.72 days	84 years
Neptune	0.67 days	164 years
Pluto	6.39 days	248 years

It seems odd that one day on Mercury equals 58.6 Earth days, while it only takes 30 more days to make a year. Each planet orbits the sun individually, and at different speeds. Therefore, one day is not the same throughout the universe.

What does all this have to do with getting "Back to Eden"? Unless you believe God is looking down on us from a cloud, we can speculate that God exists somewhere else in this universe, and it's possible the length of His day determines one day in the Genesis creation. I'm merely showing the possibility that a planet could rotate longer than what we are used to on Earth and that Earth might have rotated slower or even faster thousands of years ago. This ties into something I learned from reading the doctrines of the Latter-day Saint church years ago about God living at the center of the universe, where one rotation on his home could take a thousand years.

The biblical insight into how long a day for God is comes in 2 Peter 3:8 in the Bible, where Peter tells us that where God resides it takes 1,000 years to make a full day.

2 PETER 3:8

⁸ But, beloved, be not ignorant of this one thing, that one day is with the Lord as a thousand years, and a thousand years as one day.

However, this isn't enough for some to believe that a day with God lasts 1,000 years, since not everyone who believes in creation also believes in the doctrine of the New Testament. Therefore, what does the Old Testament say about this? Not much, other than what David writes in Psalms 90:4 when he speaks of a prayer of Moses.

PSALMS 90:4

⁴ For a thousand years in thy sight are but as yesterday
when it is past, and as a watch in the night.

I remembered something the pastor from one of the local churches said about Adam's death, that it was in God's time frame of a day. In Genesis 2:17, Adam is told *"But of the tree of the knowledge of good and evil, thou shalt not eat of it: for in the day that thou eatest thereof thou shalt surely die."* However, Adam didn't die that day. As a matter of fact, he died at the age of 930, almost 1,000 years later. Of course, there is more to this story that pertains to The Fall, when Adam and Eve ate the fruit, but I'm just pointing out the parallel of time.

The importance of establishing that Earth wasn't created according to man's understanding of a day isn't to build a bridge between God and science, or to separate people by faith. It's partly to show that the ever-evolving theories of science might actually be evolving toward what the scriptures have been saying this whole time. Most scientists claim that Earth took a long time to form, create, and evolve life into one location. Which isn't far off from what the scriptures tell us. The problem is always in the time frame.

Some categorize the story of creation as merely a story. I find the layout order in which God created things to be the key to why it's not just a story. If someone decided 7,000 or so years ago to fabricate a creation story about a beautiful Garden called Eden, they would have started with man being created first to witness it all unfold. Instead, the writing is in the same order that science claims evolution happened. Yet, it wasn't until 1744 that the idea of transmutation of species was even a thing, and Darwin didn't explain his theory of evolution until 1859. Therefore, whoever wrote the manuscript scrolls of Genesis knew the right order. God is not a God of confusion, and this is how God is science.

Back to the timeline of creation and how the gates of Eden fit into it. Could it have happened 13,000 years ago? Yes, but first I need to turn the tables to science and evaluate one of the other factors that puts religion and science at odds, radiocarbon dating, or carbon 14.

Typically, archeology claims carbon 14 (C14) dating shows that ancient cultures existed in the world longer than the parameters of God's six-day creation over 6,000 years ago. The estimate ranges between 13,000 years and 36,000 years. Yet, if we apply our theory of each creation day being closer to 1,000 Earth days, one day with God, we get closer to some of those radiocarbon dates. That gives us approximately 13,000 years (6,000 years of creation + 1,000 years of rest + over 6,000 years since Adam and Eve left the gates of Eden). This is as long as we can stretch Genesis creation, and it still doesn't explain how nuclear chemists and archeology can come up with dates of 20,000+ years. So let us break it down.

Most of us have heard the terminology of carbon 14 dating, or C14, and how it can date the age of organisms and organic material in ranges of thousands of years. Radiocarbon dating typically states only ages of 40,000 to 50,000 years, so it doesn't give us the ages of rocks. The challenge occurs when we assume radiocarbon years and calendar years are the same. This isn't always the case. In fact, you would have to have an almost perfect equilibrium of C14 production in the atmosphere to the perfect amount of organic life absorbing the C14. The next image is a basic cycle of C14.

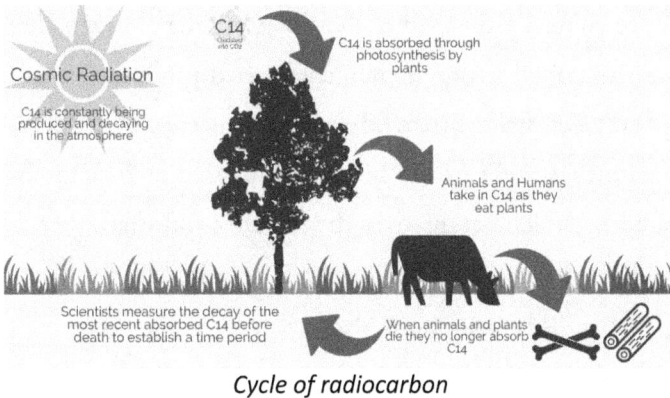

Cycle of radiocarbon

As the diagram illustrates, C14 is constantly being produced and instantly starts to decay in the atmosphere, where it is then absorbed by plants through photosynthesis. For the calibrations of carbon 14 dating to be accurate, a few assumptions are required. For starters, there needs to be a balance of plant life to absorb the constant production of C14. Also, the environment of the plant can't change its ability to absorb C14, except it does vary by hemisphere and by season, not to mention whether or not it's an aquatic plant. Studies show there have been inconsistent effects on organisms found in both freshwater and saltwater as well as human remains that live near areas where they might eat a lot of fish. This can alter the outcome of C14 dating.

There are still too many assumptions regarding the dating process to be able to state facts, especially in the balance ratios.

One thing is understood: there are new radiocarbon isotopes being created and decaying in the atmosphere constantly. The action of C14 is not in question. What is in question is the state of equilibrium. I'm sure at some point the scale was balanced, but definitely not in the beginning moments of Earth.

Hypothetically, when Earth came in contact with a solar

radioactive source, either while she was traveling through the cosmos or when she united with our Sun, she started producing C14 into her atmosphere. Yet, from either side of belief, science or religion, we can firmly state that there wasn't life on this planet at first to absorb the radiocarbon. Which means over time there would have been a lot of old C14 lingering around decaying while it waited for life to emerge. A lot of that C14 would have decayed pretty significantly, or even completely decayed into nitrogen.

Since the C14 creation is constant, it's possible to say that the older C14 would be closer to the surface of the Earth while new C14 was closer to the solar radioactive source. Which means that when life came to Earth, the C14 closer to the surfaces would have decayed to the point of almost turning into nitrogen and not been at its full testable age. This would make carbon dating results seem older than actuality. The next diagram will explain.

Cosmic Radiation

New C14   Still has for 50,000 years to decay

Old C14
Already decayed
50,000 years

Old C14
absorbed

If the most recent absorbed
C14 before death had
already decayed significantly
before absorption, the
age of the organic material
would give the wrong
dates of existence

New and old carbon 14

Also, I mentioned that freshwater and saltwater have shown significant variations in the C14 dating results; imagine what a yearlong global flood would do to C14 results. Anything found from that time period wouldn't match up, especially human remains. If archeologists ever found the bodies of people before the Flood, or even Adam and Eve, we wouldn't know based on the current calibration of radiocarbon dating. We couldn't know the unbalanced ratios that existed during the time of Eden, or after, until we could sync the C14 levels with written history. Scientists would calculate their remains to be around 48,000 years or older when they're more likely 8,000 years young.

I feel it's safe to say that the possibility of Eden fitting into the currently scientific timeline is a defining yes. Science can't prove that the C14 tests of artifacts older than recorded history are not altered by old decayed atmospheric C14, or that the other carbon isotopes in the water at the time of the Flood didn't change the age of everything older than 5,000 years.

Now, if science would use creation as a historical timeline in collaboration with radiocarbon dating, we could start to line up ancient archeological sites with a more recent timeline. That might help us understand why the people who lived there may have left. For example, until recently the Garden of Eden has been marked in places like Mesopotamia and east Africa. However, a new discovery of human bones in northwest Africa shows dates of 300,000 years old (which we know now could be extremely off if older elements affect the bones before younger elements were available). What is interesting is where the oldest bones were found.

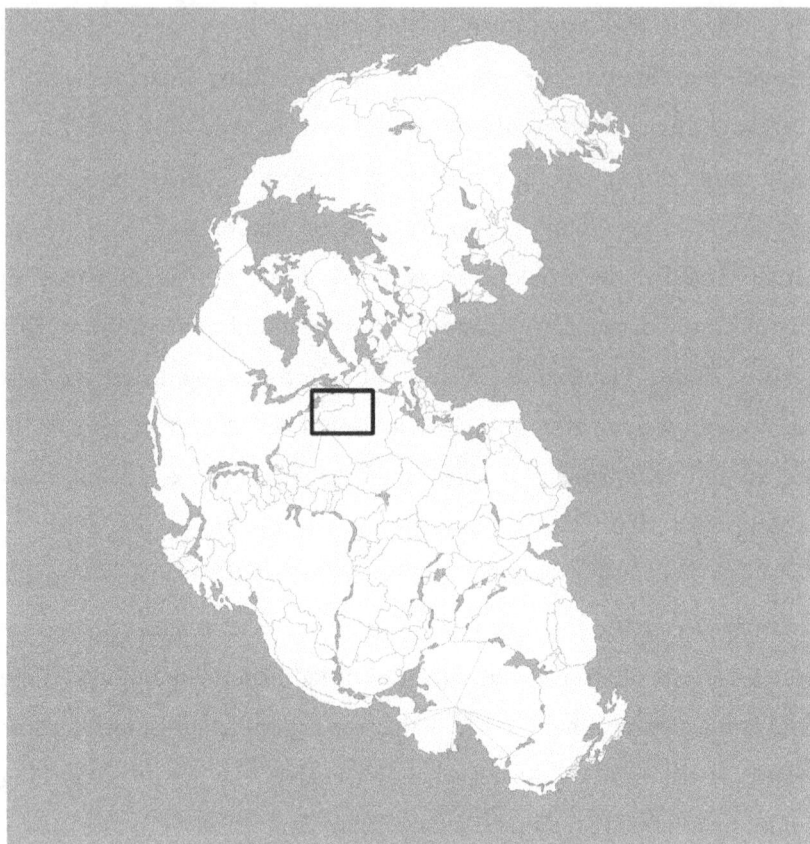

Oldest human remains found

We don't know the size of Eden, but it's safe to assume it was a pretty large area of land if Adam and Eve lived there for at least 1,000 years (the day that God rested = 1,000 years) with plants and animals while life multiplied and spread across the Earth. Therefore, if Eden was in or near North America, it's likely the bones found in northwest Africa were the bones of someone who knew the location of Eden. That's just a guess, but what isn't a guess is how places are referenced with Eden. It seems Eden was somewhere in the west, because of the references to east parts of Eden being so important. The following scriptures are examples:

GENESIS 2:8

*⁸ And the LORD God planted a garden eastward in
Eden; and there he put the man whom he had formed.*

If God planted a garden in the "eastward" part of Eden, it can be assumed that Eden extended west. So why plant a garden in the east if it was located in North America? The next image illustrates the mountains in the western part of America. To the east, at the foot of the mountains, are the plains suitable for growing crops.

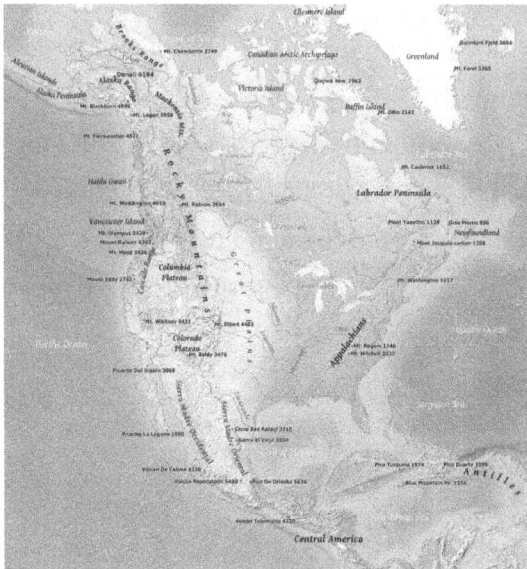

GENESIS 3:24

*²⁴ So he drove out the man; and he placed at the east
of the garden of Eden Cherubims, and a flaming sword
which turned every way, to keep the way of the tree of life.*

The tree of life was a pretty important tree, and God wanted to protect the path that led to it. I don't think we can easily walk around the Midwest of North America looking for a tree with a flaming sword and cherubims. I ponder the idea that we can't see all the things of God, and that we've lost the ability to see those things through the degeneration of our DNA.

Trees played important roles throughout the stories in the scriptures, as if they were mentioned as reference points for later generations to find places lost over time. The Garden of Eden was one of those stories told with significance to the trees. Though these next trees are not the tree of life, or the tree of good and evil, they are clues to the area. Two of the oldest trees in the world, both bristlecone pines, are found in the Inyo National Forest of California in North America, all within the projected western part of Eden. These two hardy bristlecones are both around 5,000 years old, which means they would have started growing right around the time of the Flood. The following image doesn't portray the actual oldest trees because their location in the forest is protected.

Bristlecone pine

The last verse in Genesis that gives us the direction east is about Cain, who was banished from the sight of God and away from Eden.

GENESIS 4:16

¹⁶ And Cain went out from the presence of the
LORD, and dwelt in the land of Nod, on the east of Eden.

Once again, consider the significance of "east." What was east of Eden? The land of Nod. This mysterious land was inhabited by Cain, a murderer cursed with a mark by God, who was to live out his days with his wife and his descendants. Where could he have gone? Pretty much anywhere, since we are not told anything about Nod. It's only mentioned once.

Was Nod in South Africa, where they found a complete skeleton that looked very humanlike? Or in Australia, where they found a unique humanlike skull with unusual features? Or was east of Eden in the direction of China?

Though there is no biblical support for Cain having horns and a hairy body, many tales over the years have been spun about what his cursed mark looked like. I've heard the stories since I was younger that Cain was covered in hair and left with horns to be known by others with a curse. Regardless of the validity of those old stories, it reminded me of the tale of a God worshiped ages ago in a country east of North America, the Chinese deity called Pan Gu, mentioned in a previous chapter. If you remember the image of Pan Gu, he was a hairy horned God with an uncanny resemblance to the Cain of the old tales. We don't know exactly what mark God put on Cain, but whatever it was, the people he came in contact with would know he was different.

Regardless, this small mention of Cain being sent far enough away that he wasn't near God or Eden helps solidify the idea that the boundaries of Eden didn't take over much of the land on Earth. It was a focused area that God separated from the rest of his creation, a special place to put his most significant creation, while he placed other life outside Eden.

Though it's not stated how vast Eden could have been, it is fascinating to read the clues about it:

GENESIS 2:7 – 8

7 And the LORD God formed man of the dust of the ground, and breathed into his nostrils the breath of life; and man became a living soul.

8 And the LORD God planted a garden eastward in Eden; and there he put the man whom he had formed.

GENESIS 3:23,

23 Therefore the LORD God sent him forth from the garden of Eden, to till the ground from whence he was taken.

These two scriptures flow perfectly into the theme in their own chapters, yet separately they also provide reason to think that Eden didn't take up the whole Earth and that man was not created from the dust of Eden but rather the dust from somewhere else on Earth.

God created Earth to be inhabited by man, and he created man to preserve the land along with all the life it bears. Though the lessons in Genesis tell us about the price of sin ending in death, God left clues for us to find our way back, and now we are closer to the gates of Eden.

This is not a debate, it's proof that we don't know everything there is to know about Earth, its creation, or the Garden of Eden and her hidden gate. We need to use the information from these chapters and other logical information to postulate what makes sense by the standards of both religion and science. The world and the universe are too complicated and beautifully organized to have come into existence without a higher power of knowledge guiding it.

With the words in this book, our journey toward finding Eden has merely begun. Our archeological compass points should reset to where man started, and from there we can find the other lost locations of Genesis. This book will not prove the existence of God any more than science can prove there isn't a God. Nevertheless, this book takes us back before written history and before the tarnished idea that we exist by coincidence. None of this evidence is coincidence.

A goal in writing this book was to bring to light what I had found by following the research I started at a young age, when I questioned how everything fit into God's world. I witnessed a ghost at eight, a UFO at thirteen, and the true power of both God and the Devil throughout my life. I was drawn to the mysteries God left behind, knowing there were clues that we were missing. By overlapping science and religion, the image is clearer. There should be no gap between the two, because they are one and the same. I know that's a bold and overzealous statement, but there has to be a breaking point where it all begins to make sense from all sides.

Growing up, I thought my curious mind was a curse, because no one wanted to help answer my questions about the puzzles of the Bible and how they connected to the science books I loved to read, or what happens to the soul after death, or the hovering notion of life on other worlds. Little did I know that it was God preparing my mind for a greater blessing, with answers to those questions and opening the door to much more. Since 2011, my mind has been connected with God, in constant gratitude for the lines he has drawn for me to make the connections I desired as a child. Now, I can share these pieces of the bigger puzzle with the world.

You may think we believe in different Gods, but the reality is that we believe in the same God, just in different ways. Or you may believe in an alternate version of life. Either way, this book is meant to be the beginning of a platform to expand our knowledge, so that we might find Eden. From this point I hope to engage with other minds to further research North America for evidence of a lost garden and to take a closer look at the areas surrounding Monks Mound for clues of an ark. I also want to visit the Bosnian Pyramid to help uncover more about the people who lived there. My hope is not only to bring this new information to the world to prove that these historical places existed, but also to find a path to bring together both science and religion.

Now, let our journey begin at the beginning; before the world was lost.

Resources / References

The King James Version of the Holy Bible

Evan Strong, archeologist, Australia

Richard Anderson Patterson, photographer

The Quran

The Independent and the London Evening Standard

The Encyclopedia Britannica

www.lds.org

Dr. Semir Osmanagić

Goran Marjanovic, electrical engineer

Britannica.com

Geology.com

whyislam.com

world-pyramids.com

Chinese Religion (World Religions), Mario Poceski

Author

KARISA DELAY IS an American fiction and non-fiction author who has been intrigued with the endless possibilities of the universe since childhood. Growing up, her reading interests were focused in various spiritual subjects, including religions, theories of creation, paranormal phenomenon, and extraterrestrial existence.

Her strong desire to find a connection to the world we live in by making a link between the science that tries to explain it all and the spirituality of the energy we all share has inspired her writing since 2011.

Karisa's first fiction novel, *The Crystal Gate*, was released in 2012, and her second book *Four Rivers* in 2014. Her inspiration for the first two novels in the Crystal Gate series was fueled by her years of research, enabling her to create a thrilling treasure hunt wrapped in unlikely pairings between the supernatural and science to unravel the mysteries of our world.

Immersing deeper into research to further inspire future books in her series, Karisa decided to share her real-world findings in her first non-fiction book, *Before the World Was Lost*, the first volume of the Lost World series of books diving into the mysteries of the world. Karisa is also a fluent artist, who owns her own salon and art gallery. She spends most her time off loving the life of motherhood with her four daughters alongside her husband in the valleys of the Midwest.

www.ingramcontent.com/pod-product-compliance
Lightning Source LLC
LaVergne TN
LVHW051239080426
835513LV00016B/1677